C00 17286506

EDINBUR

D0530682

Ape Shall Not Kill Ape

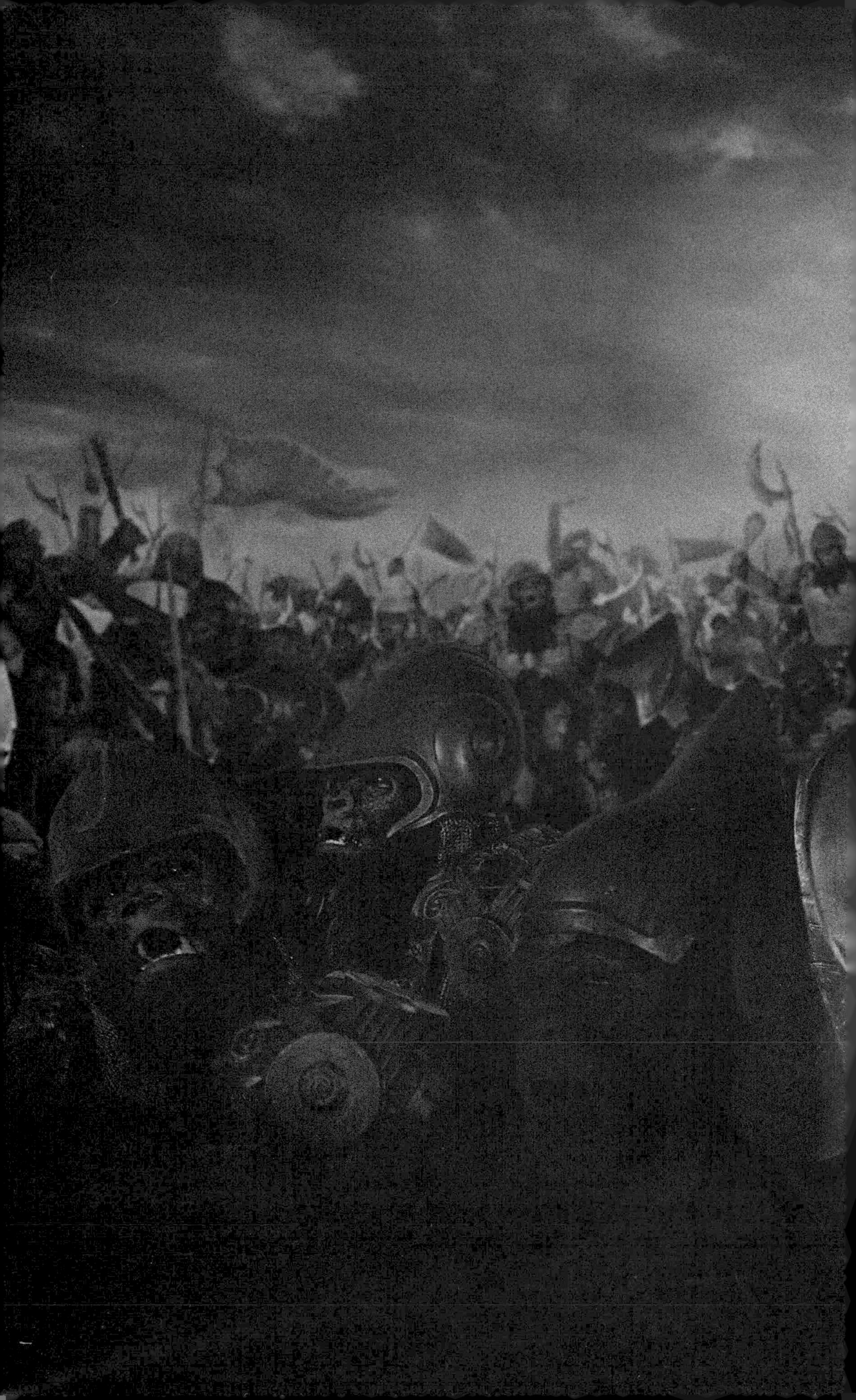

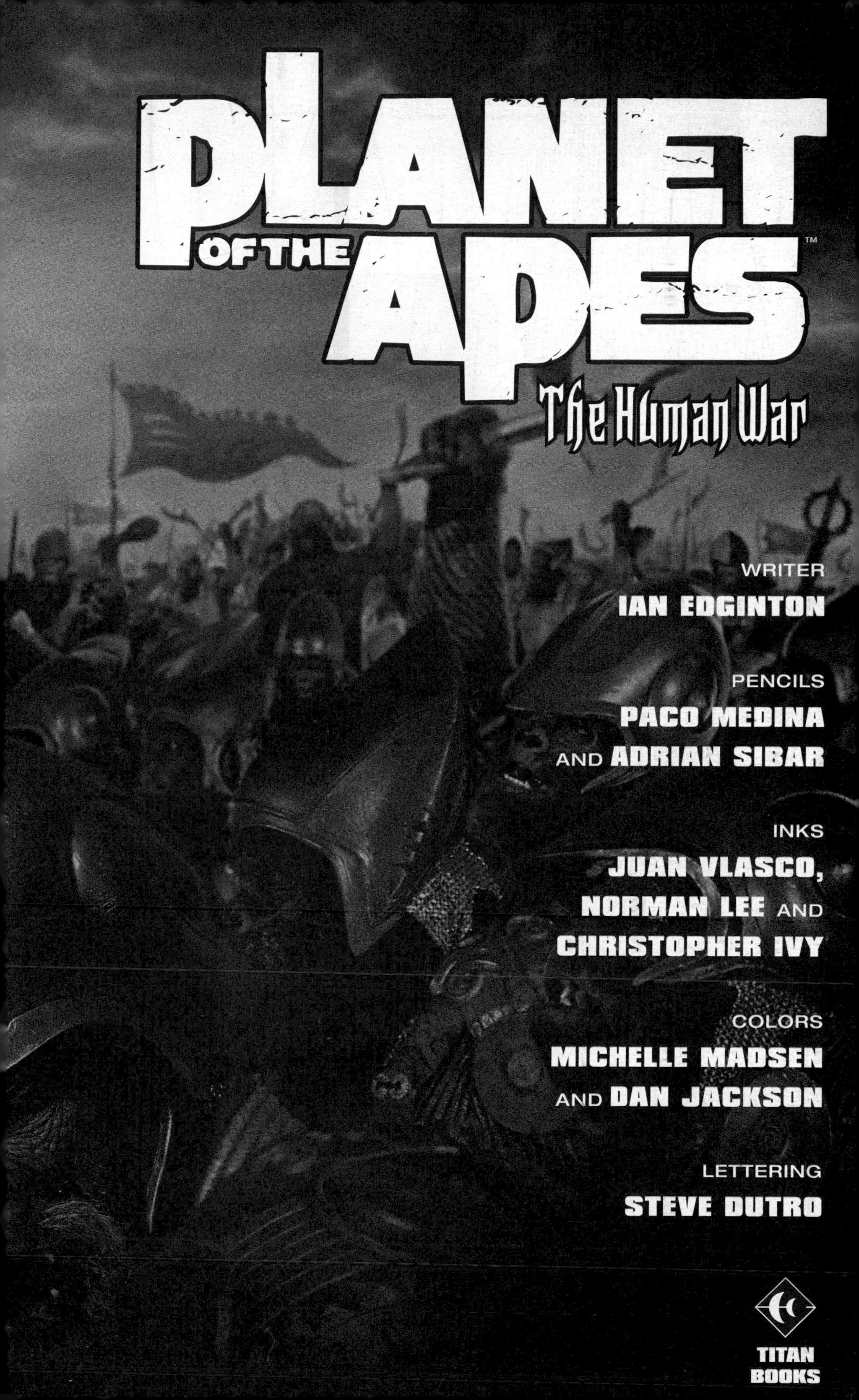

PLANET OF THE APES™

The Human War

WRITER
IAN EDGINTON

PENCILS
PACO MEDINA
AND **ADRIAN SIBAR**

INKS
JUAN VLASCO,
NORMAN LEE AND
CHRISTOPHER IVY

COLORS
MICHELLE MADSEN
AND **DAN JACKSON**

LETTERING
STEVE DUTRO

TITAN BOOKS

ORIGINAL SERIES COVERS BY
J. SCOTT CAMPBELL AND GUY MAJOR

DESIGNER
DARIN FABRICK

ASSISTANT EDITOR
PHILIP SIMON

EDITOR
PHIL AMARA

PUBLISHER
MIKE RICHARDSON

Planet of the Apes: The Human War ™ & © 2001 Twentieth Century Fox Film Corporation. All rights reserved. TM designates a trademark of Twentieth Century Fox Film Corporation.

No portion of this publication may be reproduced or transmitted, in any form or by any means, without the express written permission of the copyright holders. Names, characters, places, and incidents featured in this publication are either the product of the author's imagination or are used fictitiously. Any resemblance to actual persons (living or dead), events, institutions, or locales, without satiric intent, is coincidental.

EDINBURGH
CITY LIBRARIES
C00 1728650 6
| BFS | 12 DEC 2002 |
£6 99

PLANET OF THE APES: THE HUMAN WAR
ISBN: 1 84023 380 X

Published by Titan Books, a division of Titan Publishing Group Ltd.
144 Southwark St
London SE1 0UP

A CIP catalogue record for this title is available from the British Library.

First edition July 2001
10 9 8 7 6 5 4 3 2 1

Printed in Italy.

What did you think of this book? We love to hear from our readers.
Please email us at: readerfeedback@titanemail.com or write to us at
the above address.

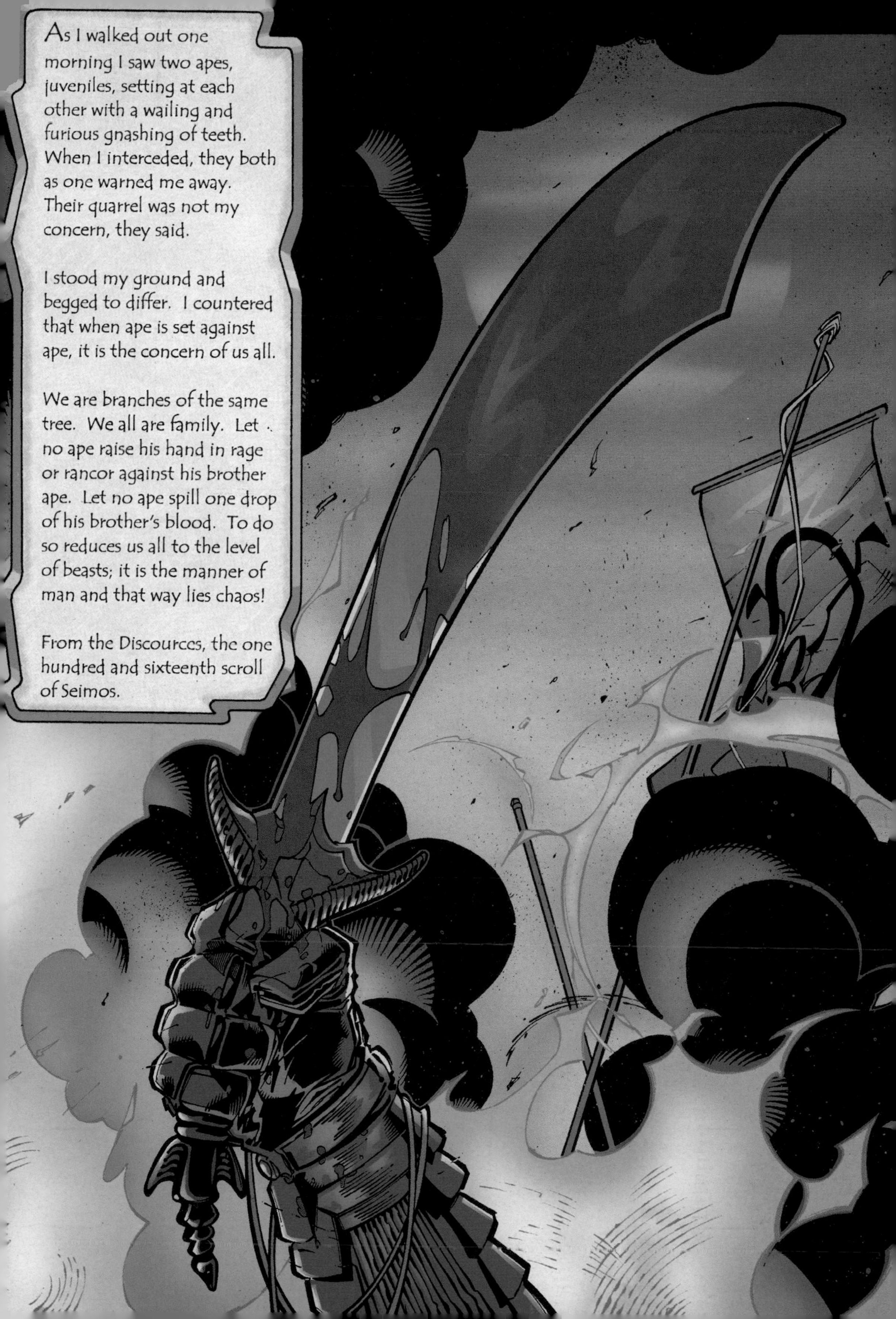
As I walked out one morning I saw two apes, juveniles, setting at each other with a wailing and furious gnashing of teeth. When I interceded, they both as one warned me away. Their quarrel was not my concern, they said.
I stood my ground and begged to differ. I countered that when ape is set against ape, it is the concern of us all.
We are branches of the same tree. We all are family. Let no ape raise his hand in rage or rancor against his brother ape. Let no ape spill one drop of his brother's blood. To do so reduces us all to the level of beasts; it is the manner of man and that way lies chaos!
From the Discources, the one hundred and sixteenth scroll of Seimos.

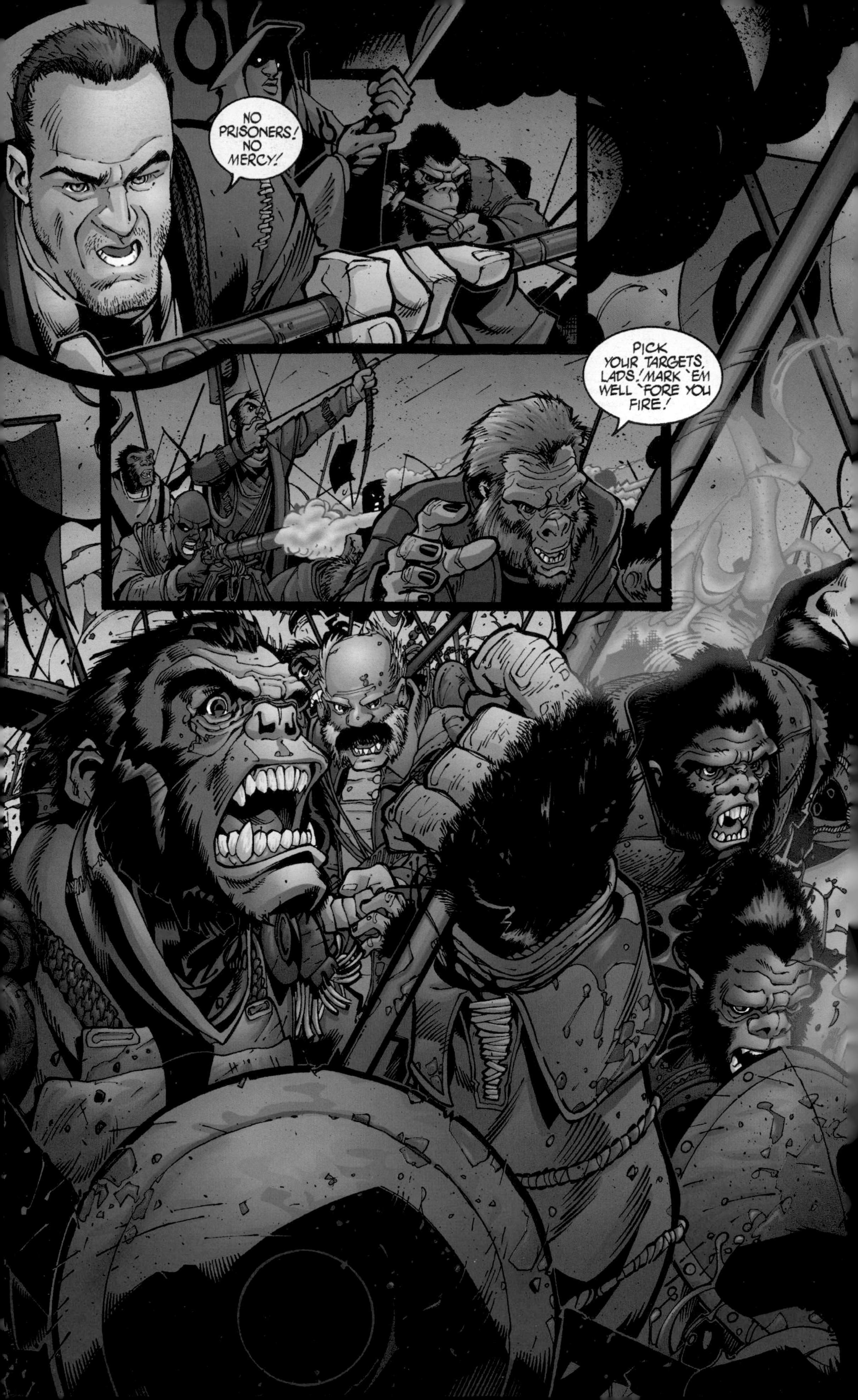
NO PRISONERS! NO MERCY!
PICK YOUR TARGETS, LADS! MARK `EM WELL `FORE YOU FIRE!

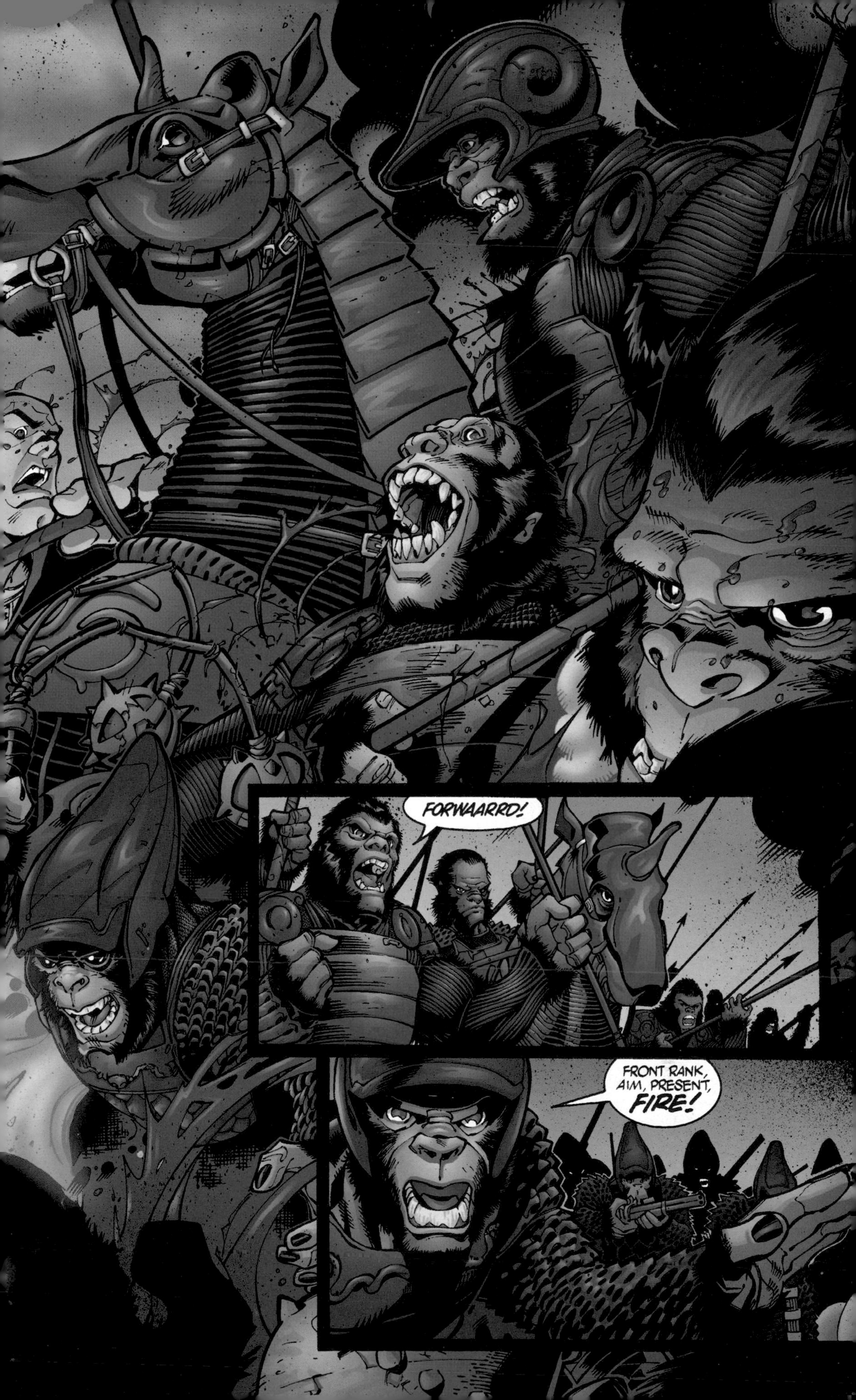
FORWAARRD!
FRONT RANK, AIM, PRESENT, FIRE!

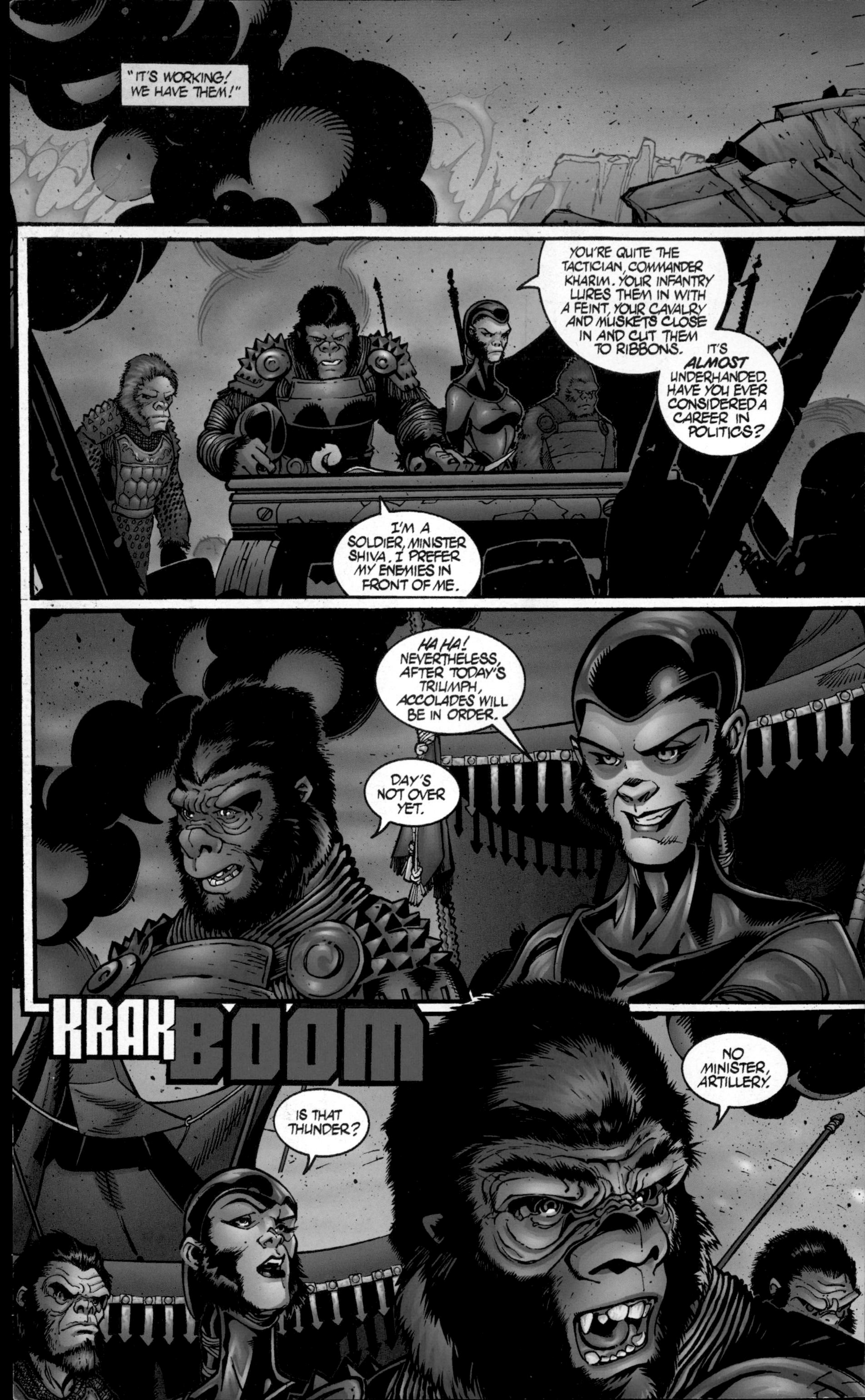
"IT'S WORKING! WE HAVE THEM!"
YOU'RE QUITE THE TACTICIAN, COMMANDER KHARIM. YOUR INFANTRY LURES THEM IN WITH A FEINT, YOUR CAVALRY AND MUSKETS CLOSE IN AND CUT THEM TO RIBBONS.
IT'S ALMOST UNDERHANDED. HAVE YOU EVER CONSIDERED A CAREER IN POLITICS?
I'M A SOLDIER, MINISTER SHIVA. I PREFER MY ENEMIES IN FRONT OF ME.
HA HA! NEVERTHELESS, AFTER TODAY'S TRIUMPH, ACCOLADES WILL BE IN ORDER.
DAY'S NOT OVER YET.
KRAK
BOOM
IS THAT THUNDER?
NO MINISTER, ARTILLERY.

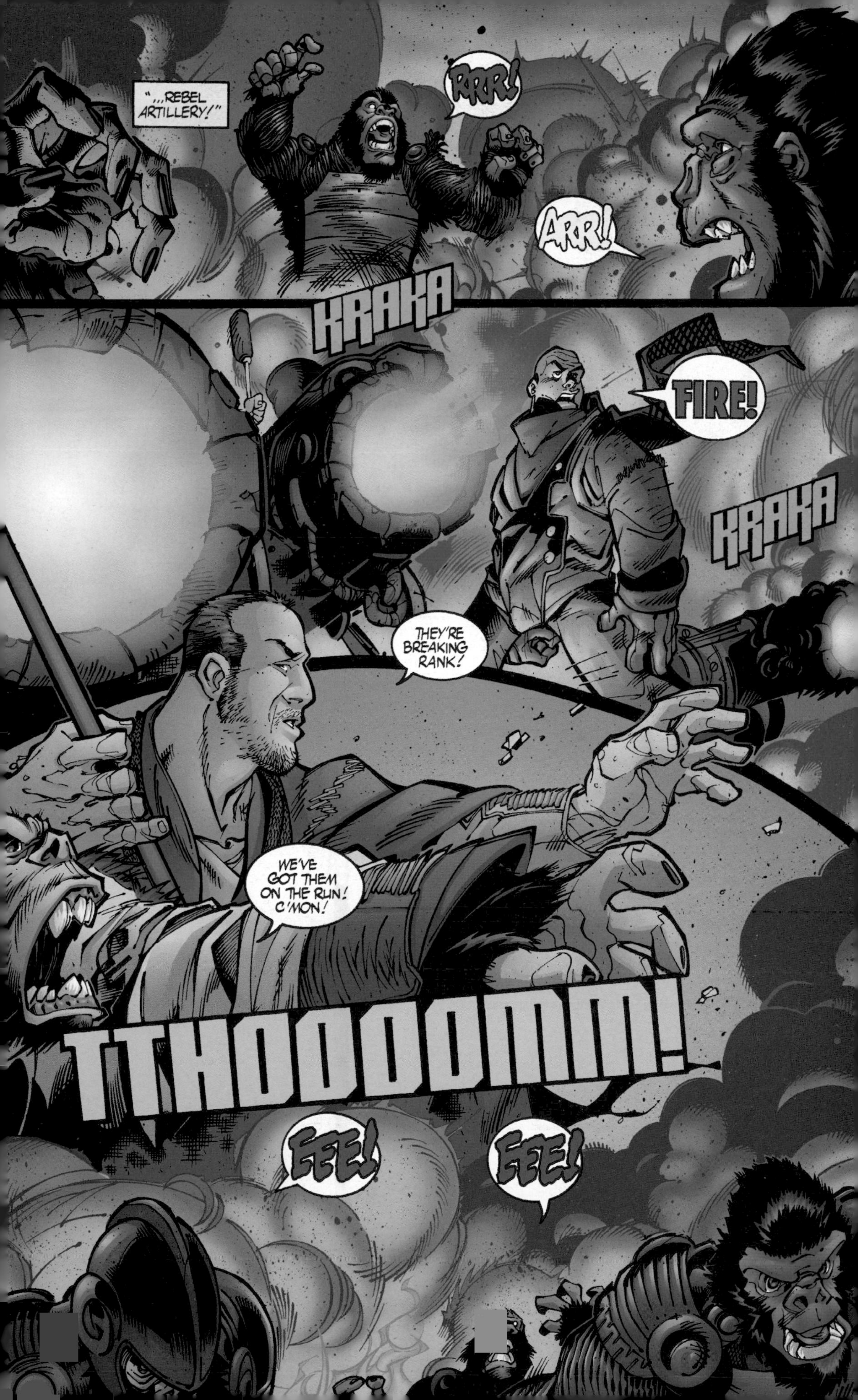
"...REBEL ARTILLERY!"
RRRR!
ARRR!
KRAKA
FIRE!
KRAKA
THEY'RE BREAKING RANK!
WE'VE GOT THEM ON THE RUN! C'MON!
TTHOOOOMM!
EEE!
EEE!

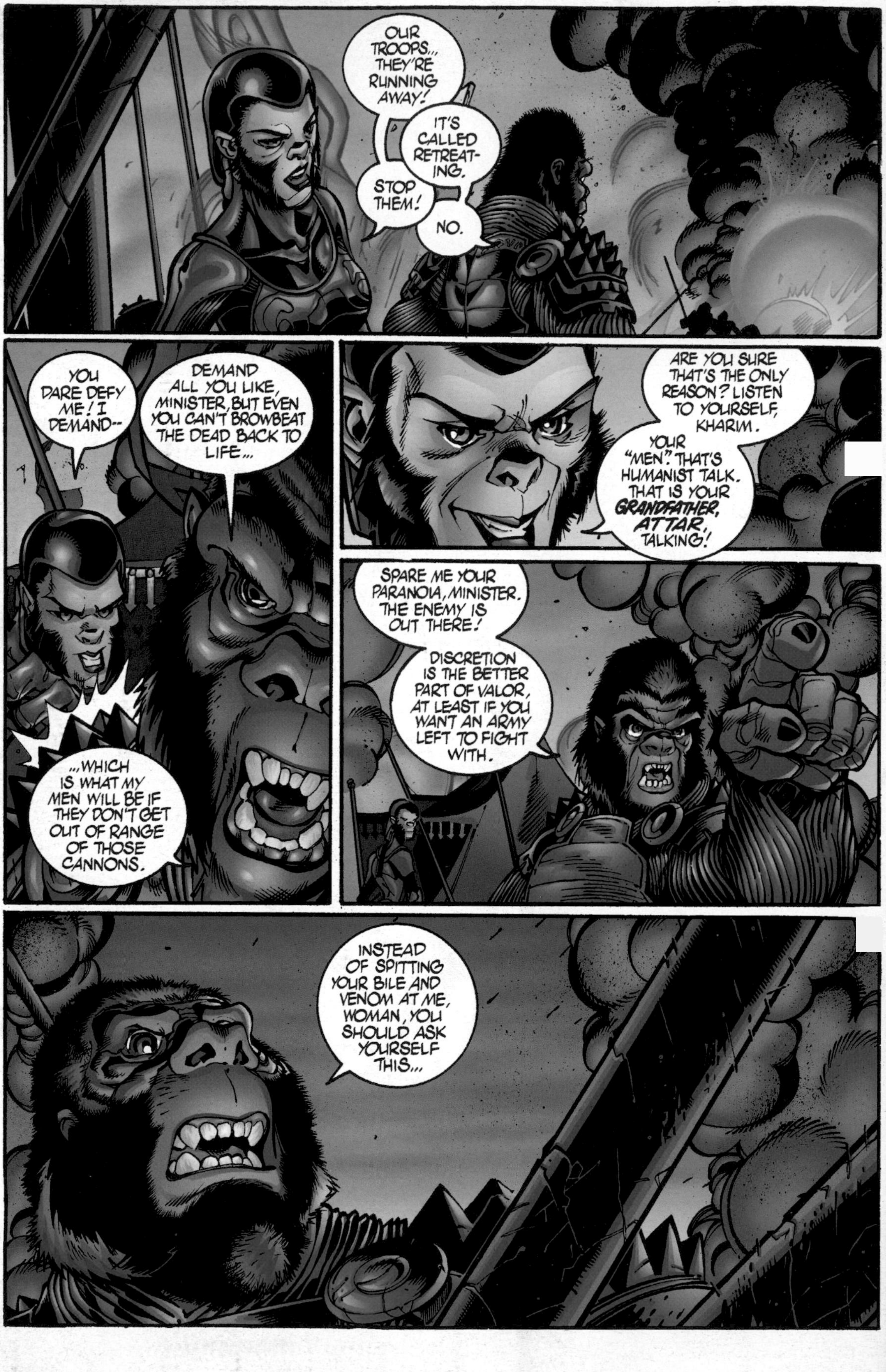
OUR TROOPS... THEY'RE RUNNING AWAY!
IT'S CALLED RETREATING.
STOP THEM!
NO.
YOU DARE DEFY ME! I DEMAND--
DEMAND ALL YOU LIKE, MINISTER, BUT EVEN YOU CAN'T BROWBEAT THE DEAD BACK TO LIFE...
...WHICH IS WHAT MY MEN WILL BE IF THEY DON'T GET OUT OF RANGE OF THOSE CANNONS.
ARE YOU SURE THAT'S THE ONLY REASON? LISTEN TO YOURSELF, KHARIM.
YOUR "MEN." THAT'S HUMANIST TALK. THAT IS YOUR GRANDFATHER, ATTAR, TALKING!
SPARE ME YOUR PARANOIA, MINISTER. THE ENEMY IS OUT THERE!
DISCRETION IS THE BETTER PART OF VALOR, AT LEAST IF YOU WANT AN ARMY LEFT TO FIGHT WITH.
INSTEAD OF SPITTING YOUR BILE AND VENOM AT ME, WOMAN, YOU SHOULD ASK YOURSELF THIS...

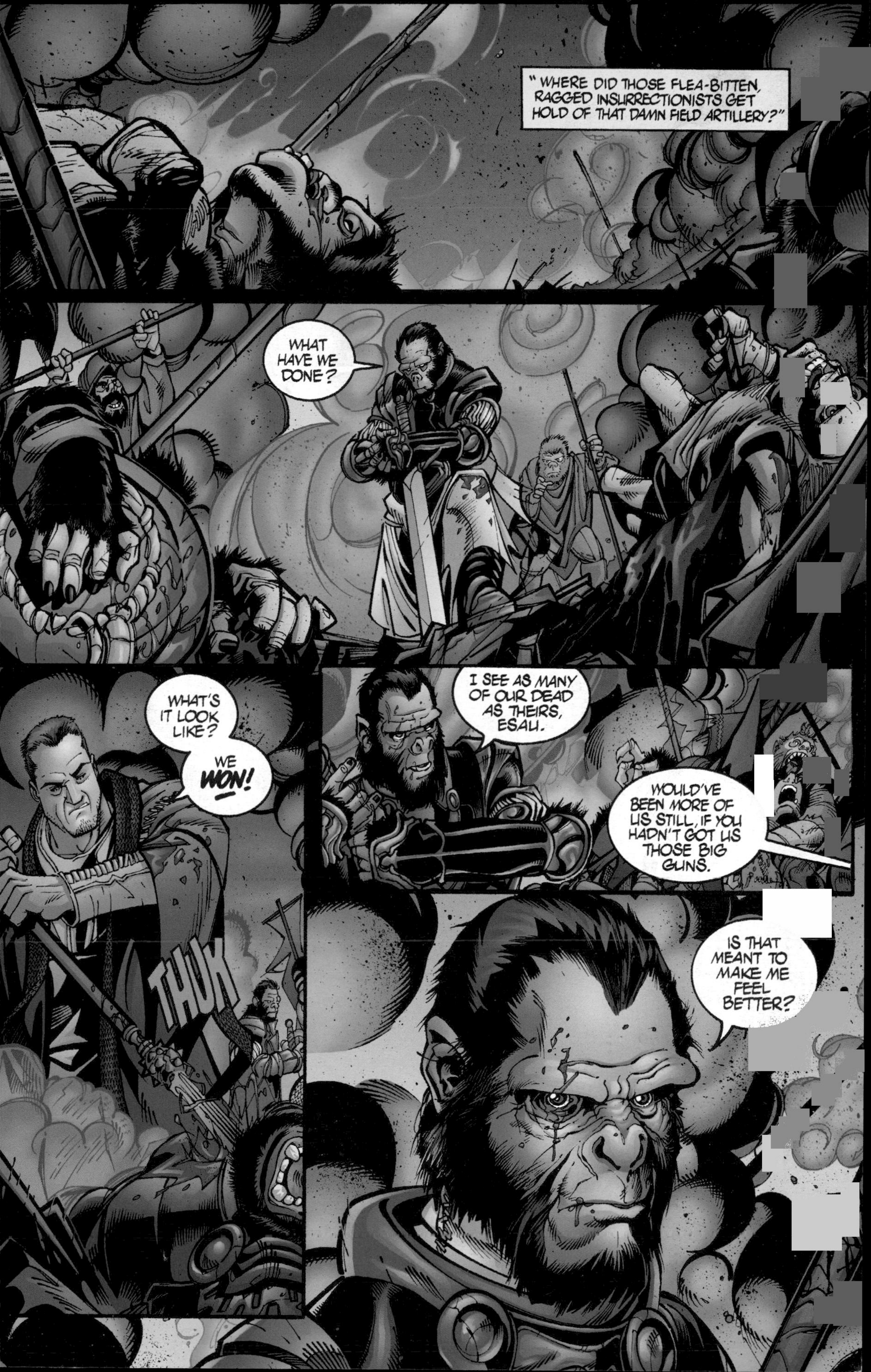
"WHERE DID THOSE FLEA-BITTEN, RAGGED INSURRECTIONISTS GET HOLD OF THAT DAMN FIELD ARTILLERY?"
WHAT HAVE WE DONE?
WHAT'S IT LOOK LIKE?
WE WON!
I SEE AS MANY OF OUR DEAD AS THEIRS, ESAU.
WOULD'VE BEEN MORE OF US STILL, IF YOU HADN'T GOT US THOSE BIG GUNS.
THUK
IS THAT MEANT TO MAKE ME FEEL BETTER?

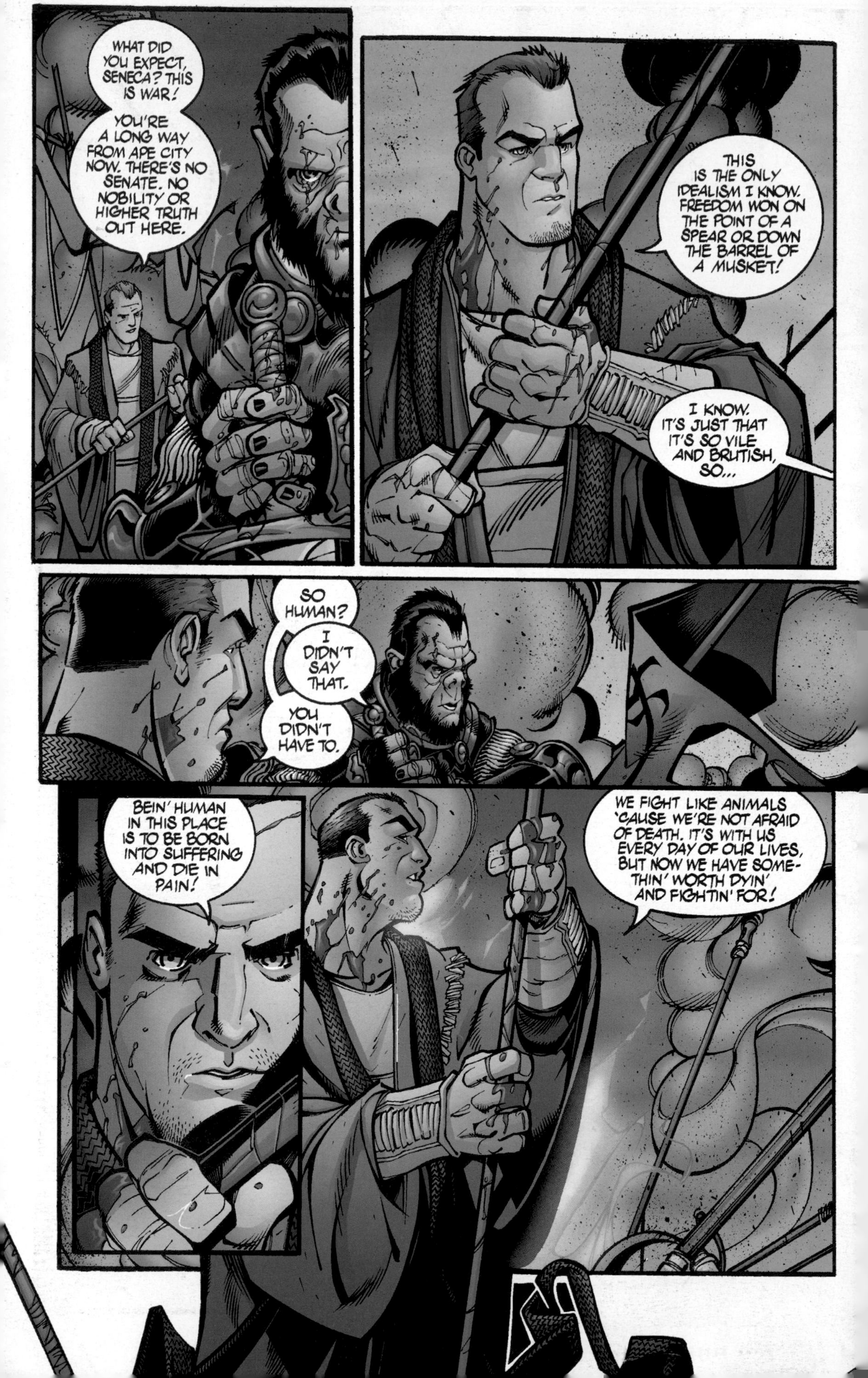
WHAT DID YOU EXPECT, SENECA? THIS IS WAR!
YOU'RE A LONG WAY FROM APE CITY NOW. THERE'S NO SENATE. NO NOBILITY OR HIGHER TRUTH OUT HERE.
THIS IS THE ONLY IDEALISM I KNOW. FREEDOM WON ON THE POINT OF A SPEAR OR DOWN THE BARREL OF A MUSKET!
I KNOW. IT'S JUST THAT IT'S SO VILE AND BRUTISH, SO...
SO HUMAN?
I DIDN'T SAY THAT.
YOU DIDN'T HAVE TO.
BEIN' HUMAN IN THIS PLACE IS TO BE BORN INTO SUFFERING AND DIE IN PAIN!
WE FIGHT LIKE ANIMALS 'CAUSE WE'RE NOT AFRAID OF DEATH. IT'S WITH US EVERY DAY OF OUR LIVES, BUT NOW WE HAVE SOME-THIN' WORTH DYIN' AND FIGHTIN' FOR!

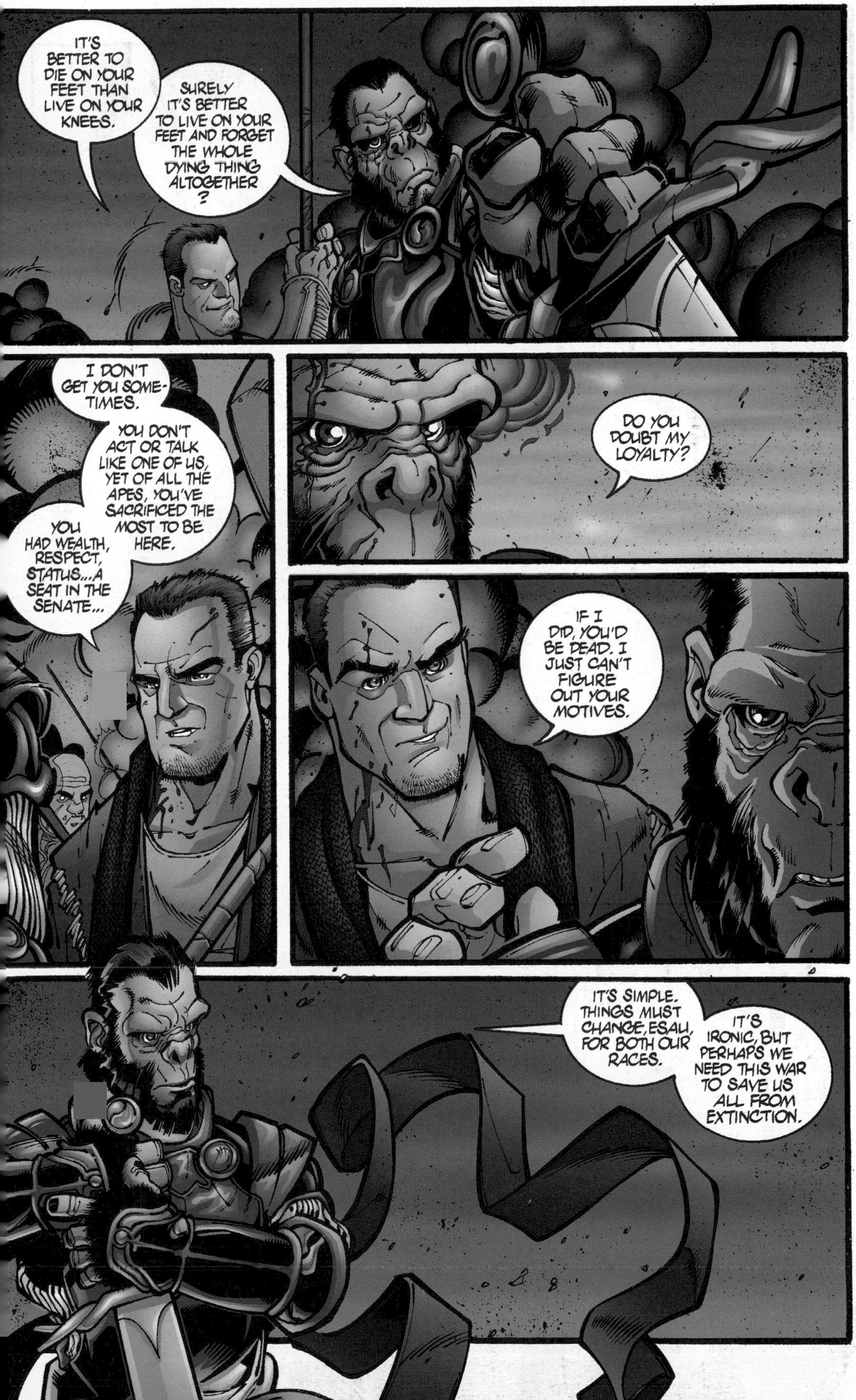
IT'S BETTER TO DIE ON YOUR FEET THAN LIVE ON YOUR KNEES.
SURELY IT'S BETTER TO LIVE ON YOUR FEET AND FORGET THE WHOLE DYING THING ALTOGETHER?
I DON'T GET YOU SOME-TIMES.
YOU DON'T ACT OR TALK LIKE ONE OF US, YET OF ALL THE APES, YOU'VE SACRIFICED THE MOST TO BE HERE.
YOU HAD WEALTH, RESPECT, STATUS...A SEAT IN THE SENATE...
DO YOU DOUBT MY LOYALTY?
IF I DID, YOU'D BE DEAD. I JUST CAN'T FIGURE OUT YOUR MOTIVES.
IT'S SIMPLE. THINGS MUST CHANGE, ESAU, FOR BOTH OUR RACES.
IT'S IRONIC, BUT PERHAPS WE NEED THIS WAR TO SAVE US ALL FROM EXTINCTION.

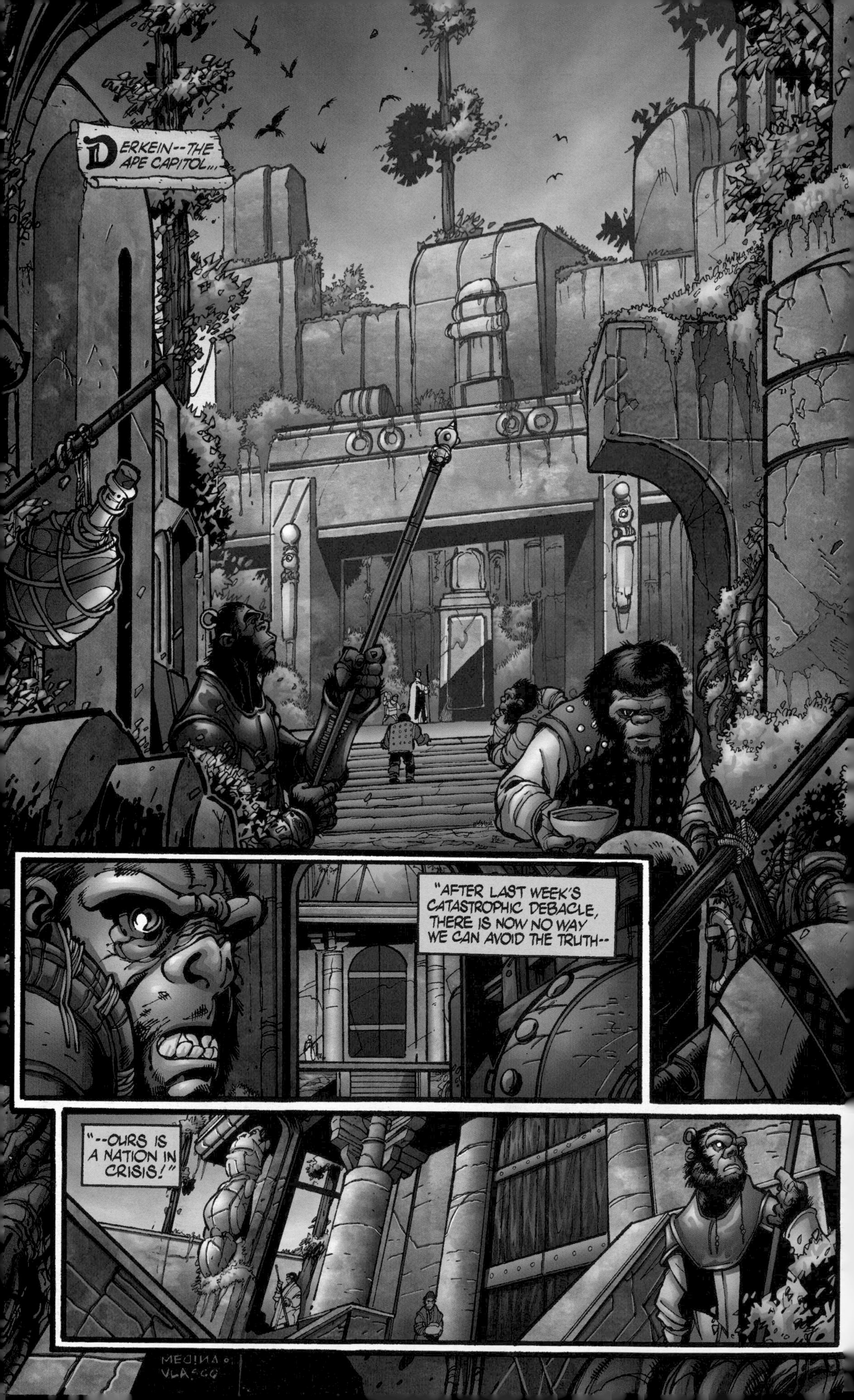
DERKEIN--THE APE CAPITOL...
"AFTER LAST WEEK'S CATASTROPHIC DEBACLE, THERE IS NOW NO WAY WE CAN AVOID THE TRUTH--
"--OURS IS A NATION IN CRISIS!"

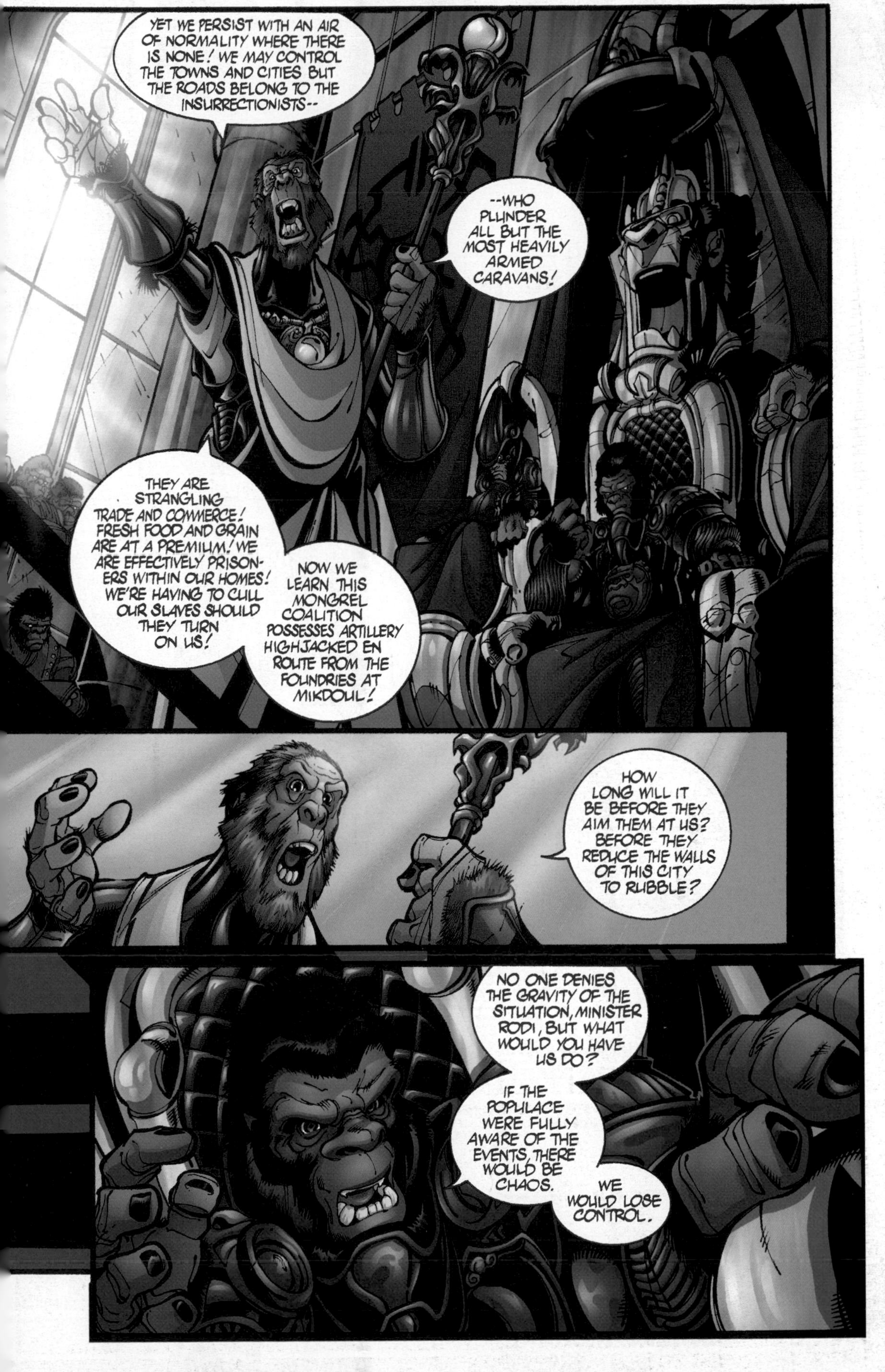
YET WE PERSIST WITH AN AIR OF NORMALITY WHERE THERE IS NONE! WE MAY CONTROL THE TOWNS AND CITIES BUT THE ROADS BELONG TO THE INSURRECTIONISTS--
--WHO PLUNDER ALL BUT THE MOST HEAVILY ARMED CARAVANS!
THEY ARE STRANGLING TRADE AND COMMERCE! FRESH FOOD AND GRAIN ARE AT A PREMIUM! WE ARE EFFECTIVELY PRISONERS WITHIN OUR HOMES! WE'RE HAVING TO CULL OUR SLAVES SHOULD THEY TURN ON US!
NOW WE LEARN THIS MONGREL COALITION POSSESSES ARTILLERY HIGHJACKED EN ROUTE FROM THE FOUNDRIES AT MIKDOUL!
HOW LONG WILL IT BE BEFORE THEY AIM THEM AT US? BEFORE THEY REDUCE THE WALLS OF THIS CITY TO RUBBLE?
NO ONE DENIES THE GRAVITY OF THE SITUATION, MINISTER RODI, BUT WHAT WOULD YOU HAVE US DO?
IF THE POPULACE WERE FULLY AWARE OF THE EVENTS, THERE WOULD BE CHAOS.
WE WOULD LOSE CONTROL.

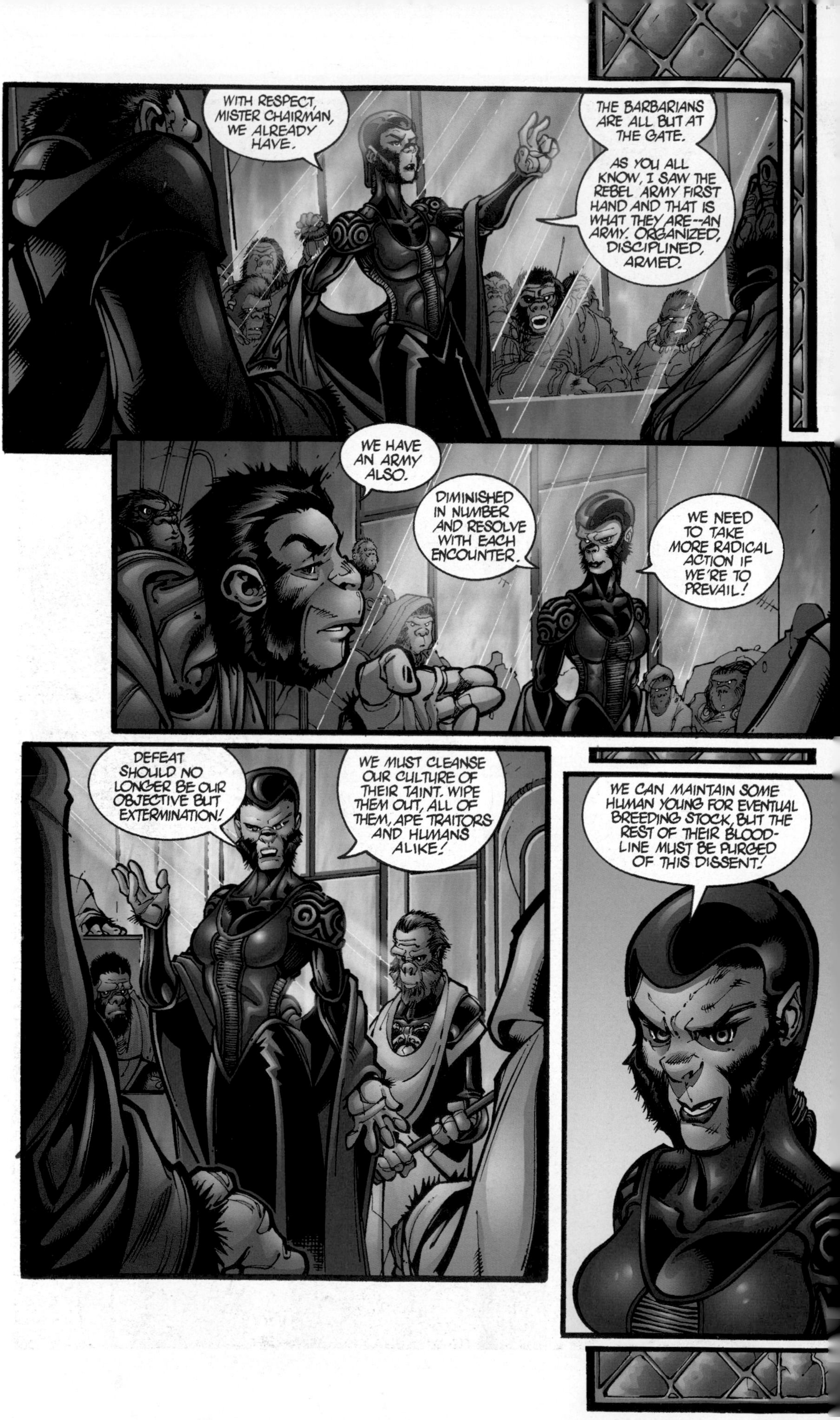

WITH RESPECT, MISTER CHAIRMAN, WE ALREADY HAVE.
THE BARBARIANS ARE ALL BUT AT THE GATE.
AS YOU ALL KNOW, I SAW THE REBEL ARMY FIRST HAND AND THAT IS WHAT THEY ARE--AN ARMY. ORGANIZED, DISCIPLINED, ARMED.
WE HAVE AN ARMY ALSO.
DIMINISHED IN NUMBER AND RESOLVE WITH EACH ENCOUNTER.
WE NEED TO TAKE MORE RADICAL ACTION IF WE'RE TO PREVAIL!
DEFEAT SHOULD NO LONGER BE OUR OBJECTIVE BUT EXTERMINATION!
WE MUST CLEANSE OUR CULTURE OF THEIR TAINT. WIPE THEM OUT, ALL OF THEM, APE TRAITORS AND HUMANS ALIKE!
WE CAN MAINTAIN SOME HUMAN YOUNG FOR EVENTUAL BREEDING STOCK, BUT THE REST OF THEIR BLOOD-LINE MUST BE PURGED OF THIS DISSENT!

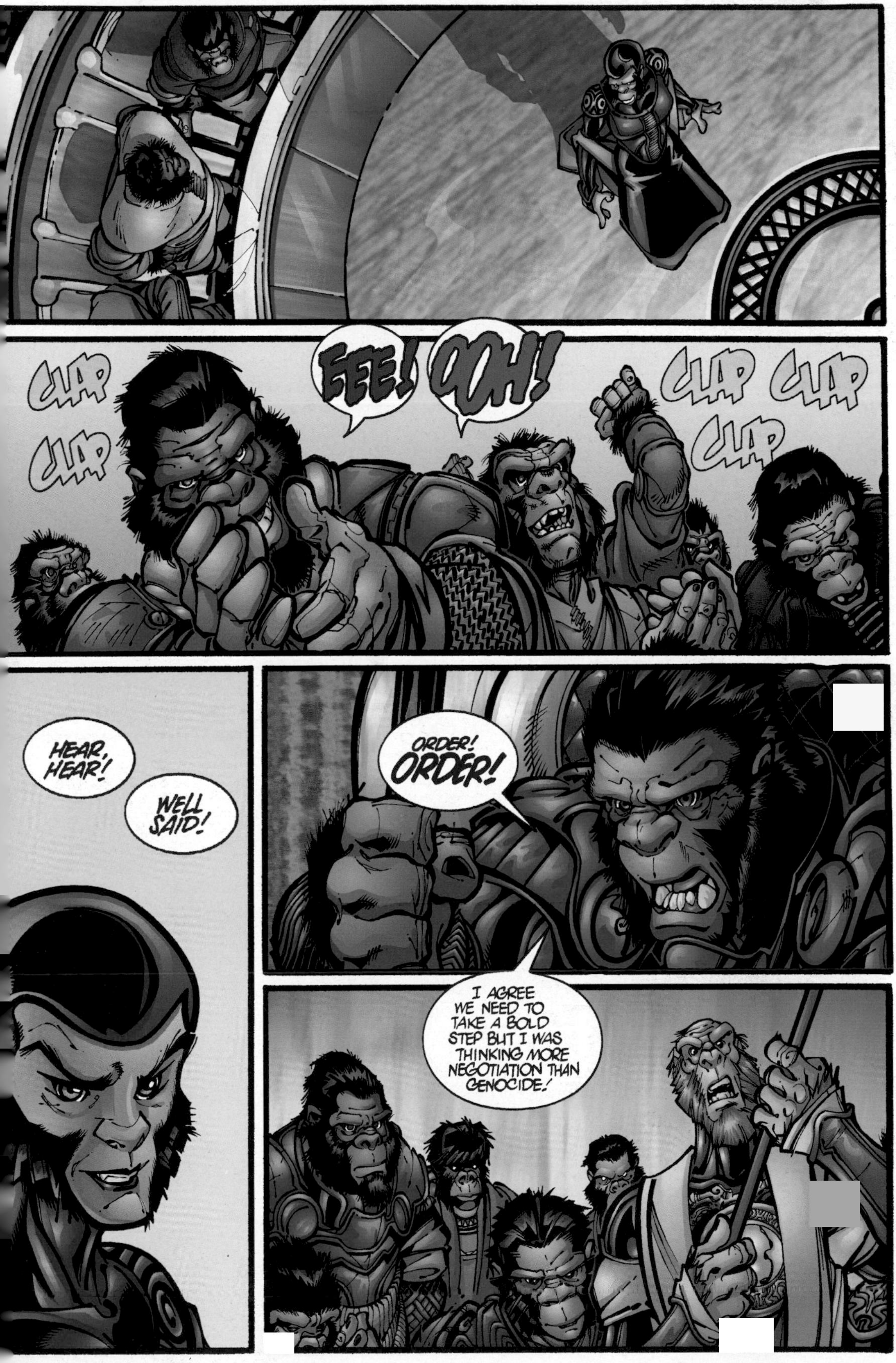
CLAP
CLAP
EEE!
OOH!
CLAP CLAP
CLAP
HEAR, HEAR!
WELL SAID!
ORDER! ORDER!
I AGREE WE NEED TO TAKE A BOLD STEP BUT I WAS THINKING MORE NEGOTIATION THAN GENOCIDE!

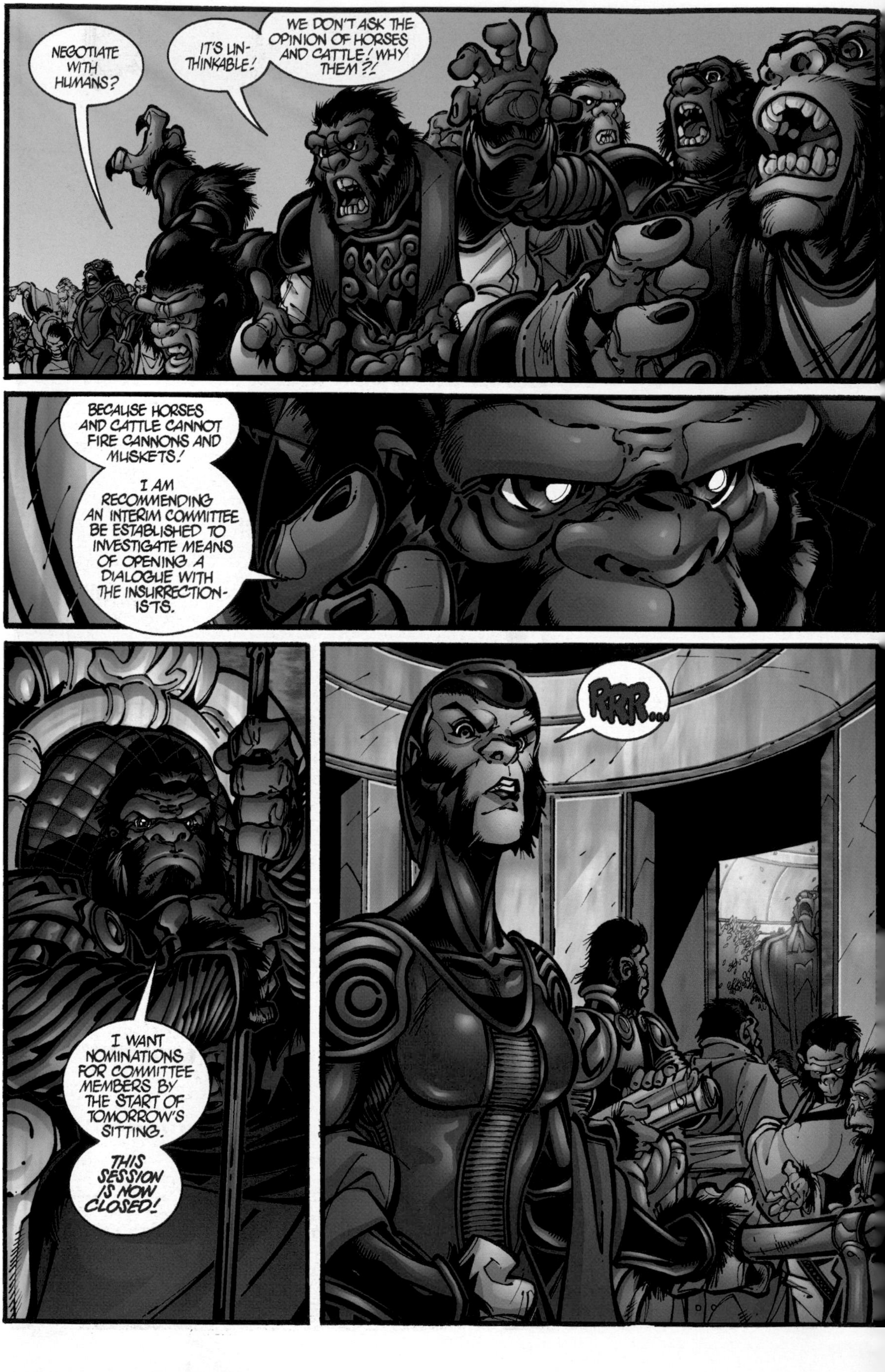
NEGOTIATE WITH HUMANS?
IT'S UN-THINKABLE!
WE DON'T ASK THE OPINION OF HORSES AND CATTLE! WHY THEM?!
BECAUSE HORSES AND CATTLE CANNOT FIRE CANNONS AND MUSKETS!
I AM RECOMMENDING AN INTERIM COMMITTEE BE ESTABLISHED TO INVESTIGATE MEANS OF OPENING A DIALOGUE WITH THE INSURRECTION-ISTS.
I WANT NOMINATIONS FOR COMMITTEE MEMBERS BY THE START OF TOMORROW'S SITTING.
THIS SESSION IS NOW CLOSED!
RRRR...

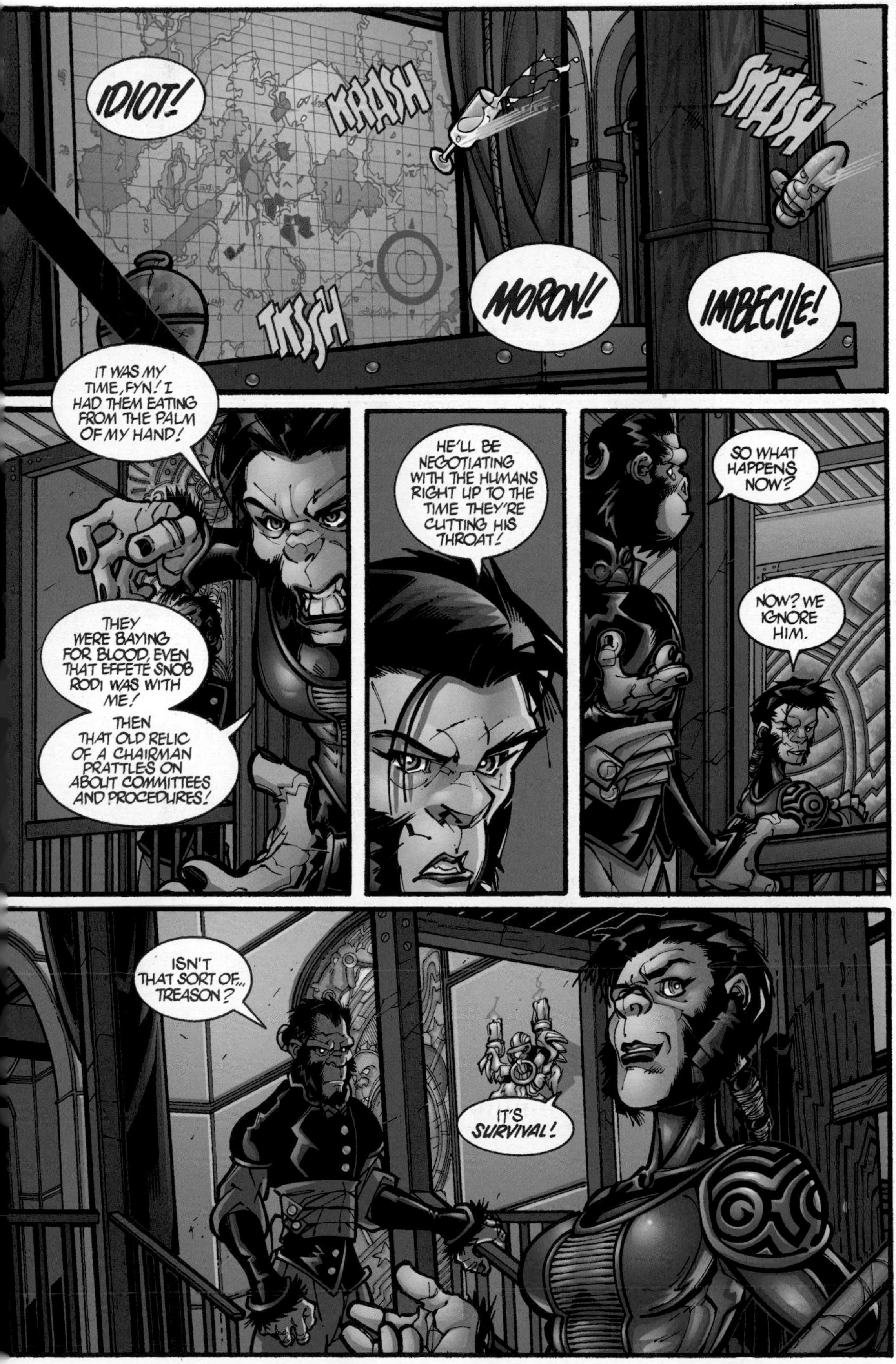
IDIOT!
KRASH
SMASH
TKSSH
MORON!
IMBECILE!
IT WAS MY TIME, FYN! I HAD THEM EATING FROM THE PALM OF MY HAND!
THEY WERE BAYING FOR BLOOD. EVEN THAT EFFETE SNOB RODI WAS WITH ME!
THEN THAT OLD RELIC OF A CHAIRMAN PRATTLES ON ABOUT COMMITTEES AND PROCEDURES!
HE'LL BE NEGOTIATING WITH THE HUMANS RIGHT UP TO THE TIME THEY'RE CUTTING HIS THROAT!
SO WHAT HAPPENS NOW?
NOW? WE IGNORE HIM.
ISN'T THAT SORT OF... TREASON?
IT'S SURVIVAL!

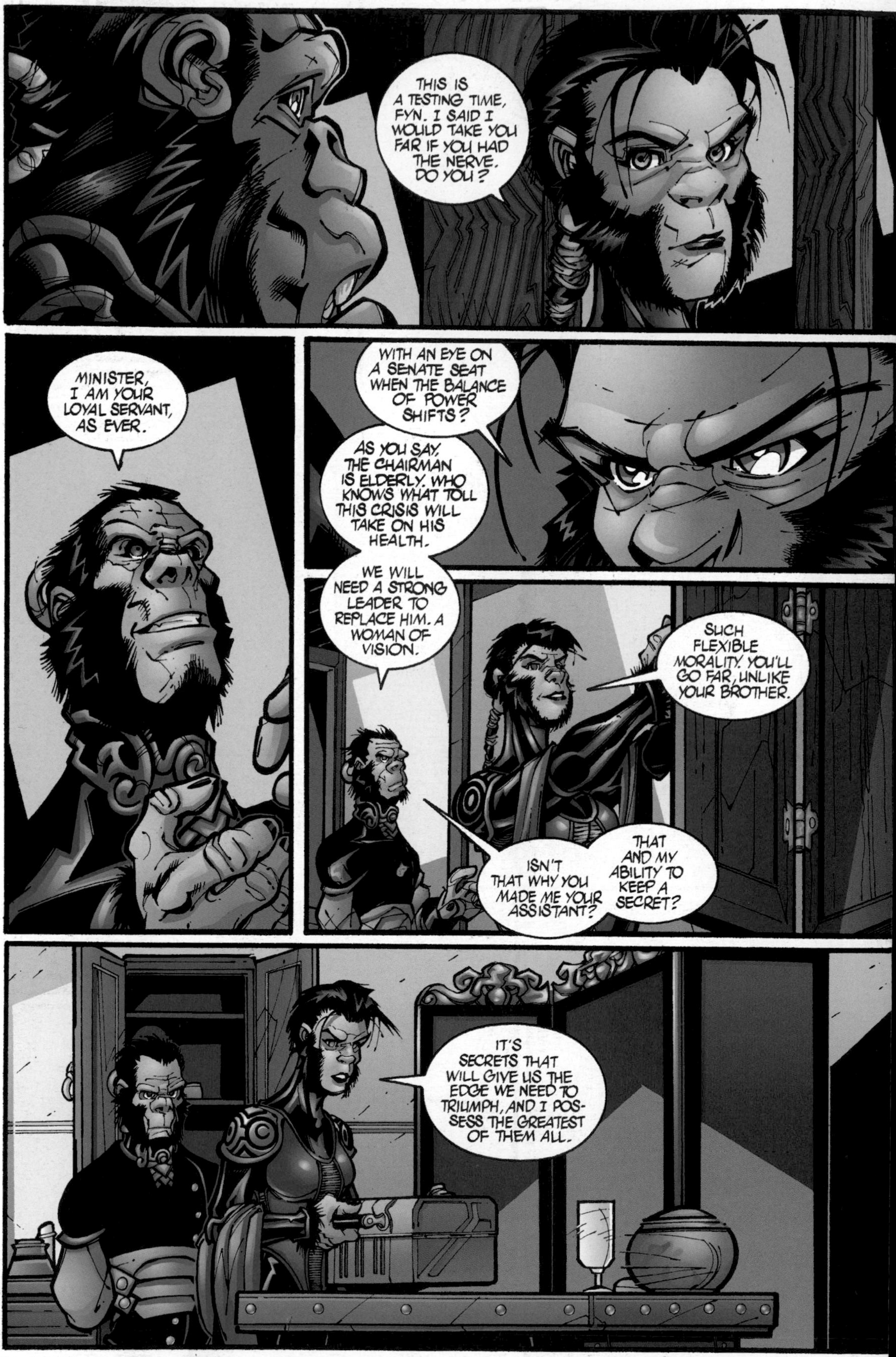
THIS IS A TESTING TIME, FYN. I SAID I WOULD TAKE YOU FAR IF YOU HAD THE NERVE. DO YOU?
MINISTER, I AM YOUR LOYAL SERVANT, AS EVER.
WITH AN EYE ON A SENATE SEAT WHEN THE BALANCE OF POWER SHIFTS?
AS YOU SAY, THE CHAIRMAN IS ELDERLY. WHO KNOWS WHAT TOLL THIS CRISIS WILL TAKE ON HIS HEALTH.
WE WILL NEED A STRONG LEADER TO REPLACE HIM. A WOMAN OF VISION.
SUCH FLEXIBLE MORALITY. YOU'LL GO FAR, UNLIKE YOUR BROTHER.
ISN'T THAT WHY YOU MADE ME YOUR ASSISTANT?
THAT AND MY ABILITY TO KEEP A SECRET?
IT'S SECRETS THAT WILL GIVE US THE EDGE WE NEED TO TRIUMPH, AND I POSSESS THE GREATEST OF THEM ALL.

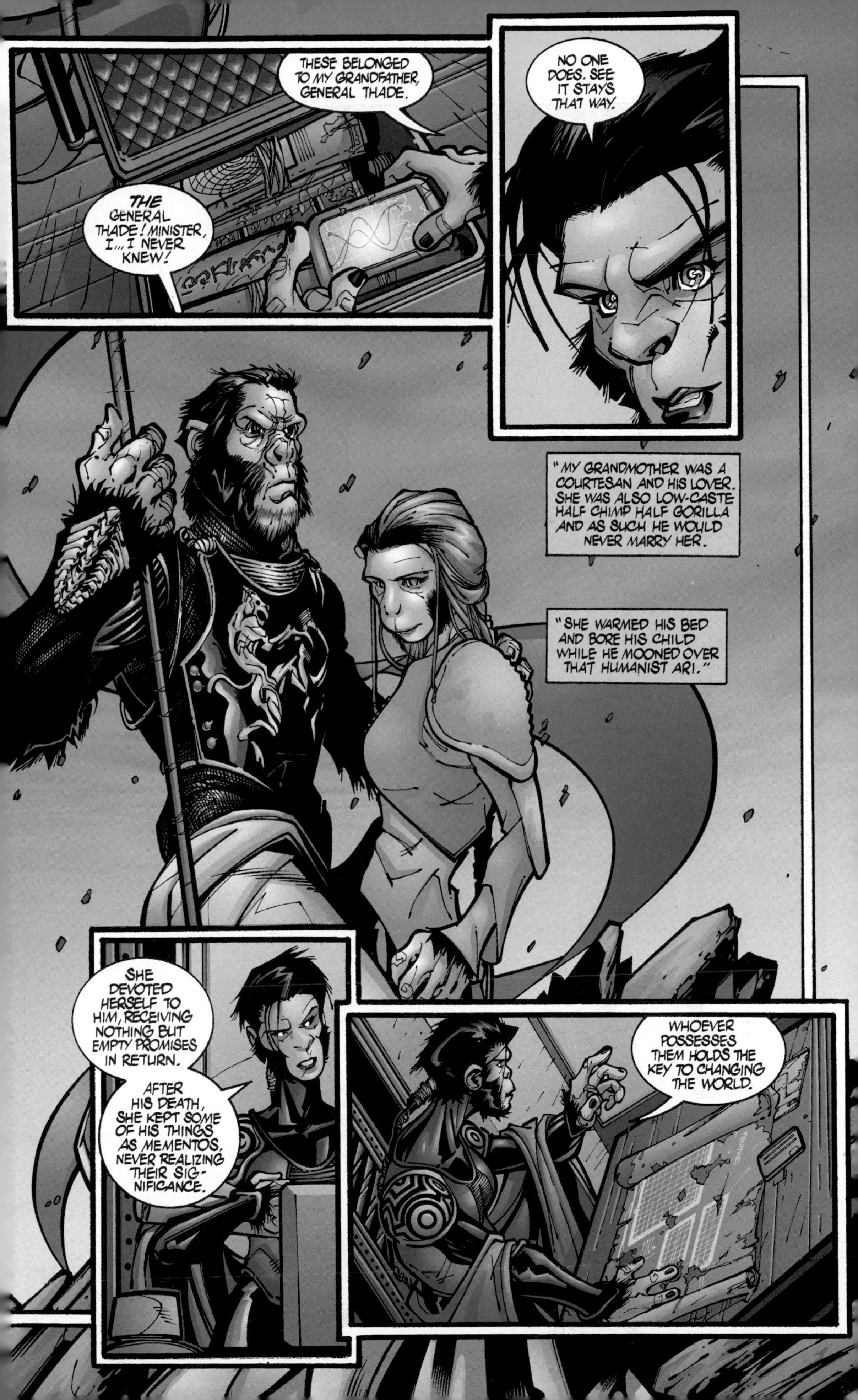
THESE BELONGED TO MY GRANDFATHER, GENERAL THADE.
THE GENERAL THADE! MINISTER, I..., I NEVER KNEW!
NO ONE DOES. SEE IT STAYS THAT WAY.
"MY GRANDMOTHER WAS A COURTESAN AND HIS LOVER. SHE WAS ALSO LOW-CASTE HALF CHIMP HALF GORILLA AND AS SUCH HE WOULD NEVER MARRY HER.
"SHE WARMED HIS BED AND BORE HIS CHILD WHILE HE MOONED OVER THAT HUMANIST ARI."
SHE DEVOTED HERSELF TO HIM, RECEIVING NOTHING BUT EMPTY PROMISES IN RETURN.
AFTER HIS DEATH, SHE KEPT SOME OF HIS THINGS AS MEMENTOS, NEVER REALIZING THEIR SIG-NIFICANCE.
WHOEVER POSSESSES THEM HOLDS THE KEY TO CHANGING THE WORLD.

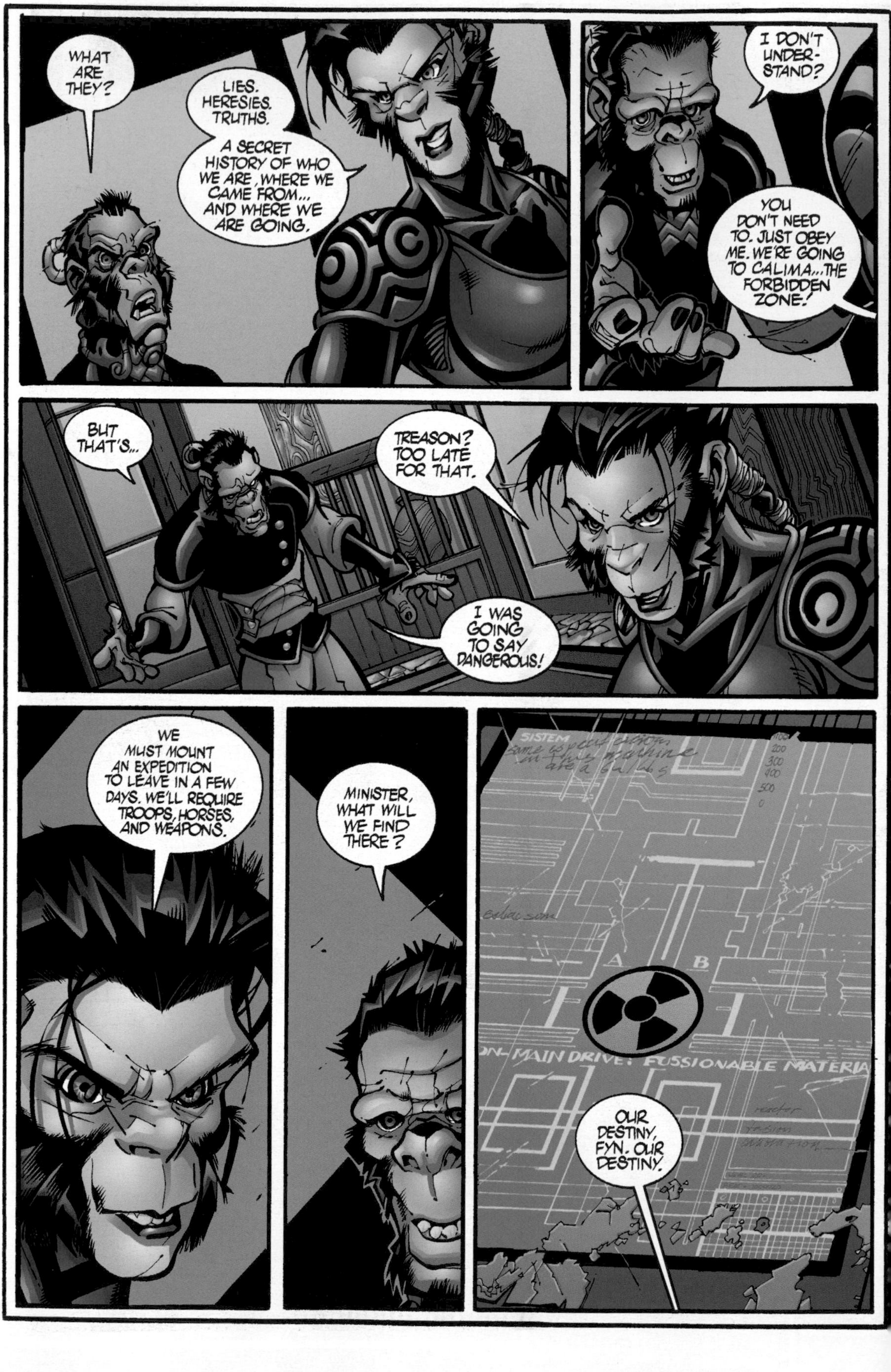
WHAT ARE THEY?
LIES. HERESIES. TRUTHS.
A SECRET HISTORY OF WHO WE ARE, WHERE WE CAME FROM... AND WHERE WE ARE GOING.
I DON'T UNDER-STAND?
YOU DON'T NEED TO. JUST OBEY ME. WE'RE GOING TO CALIMA...THE FORBIDDEN ZONE!
BUT THAT'S...
TREASON? TOO LATE FOR THAT.
I WAS GOING TO SAY DANGEROUS!
WE MUST MOUNT AN EXPEDITION TO LEAVE IN A FEW DAYS. WE'LL REQUIRE TROOPS, HORSES, AND WEAPONS.
MINISTER, WHAT WILL WE FIND THERE?
SISTEM
A
B
ON-MAIN DRIVE: FUSSIONABLE MATERIA
OUR DESTINY, FYN. OUR DESTINY.

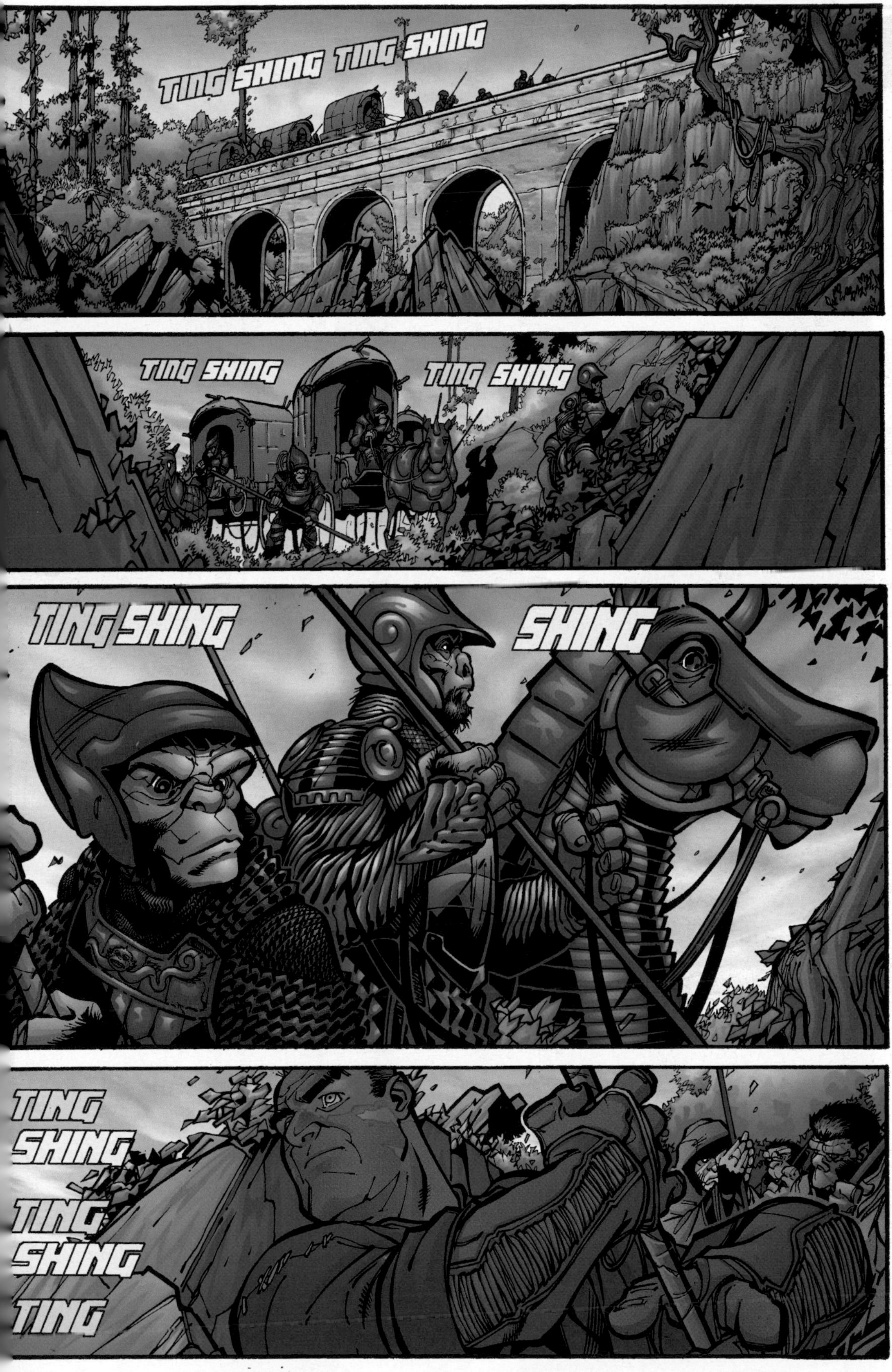
TING SHING TING SHING
TING SHING
TING SHING
TING SHING
SHING
TING
SHING
TING
SHING
TING

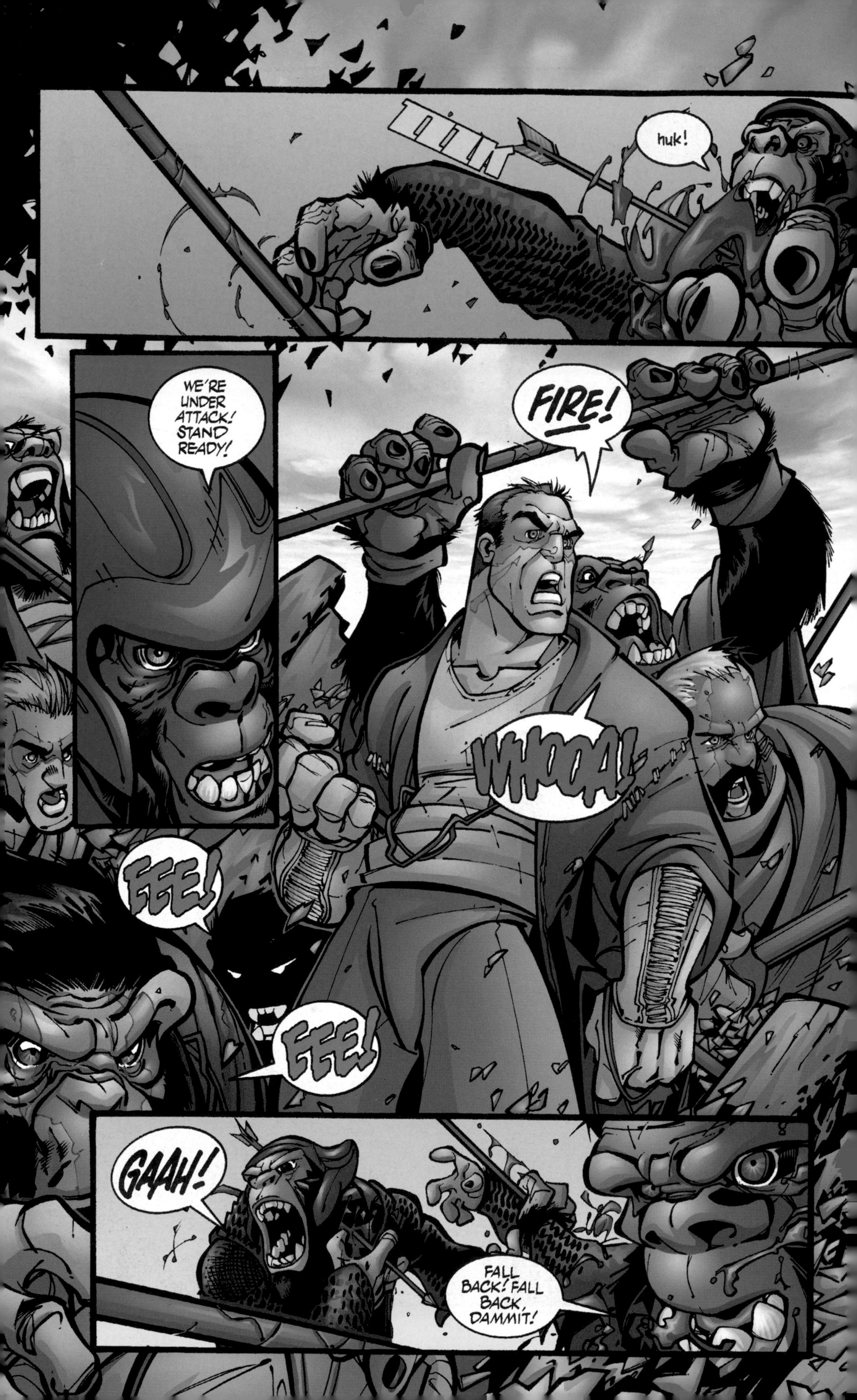
huk!
WE'RE UNDER ATTACK! STAND READY!
FIRE!
WHOOA!
EEE!
EEE!
GAAH!
FALL BACK! FALL BACK, DAMMIT!

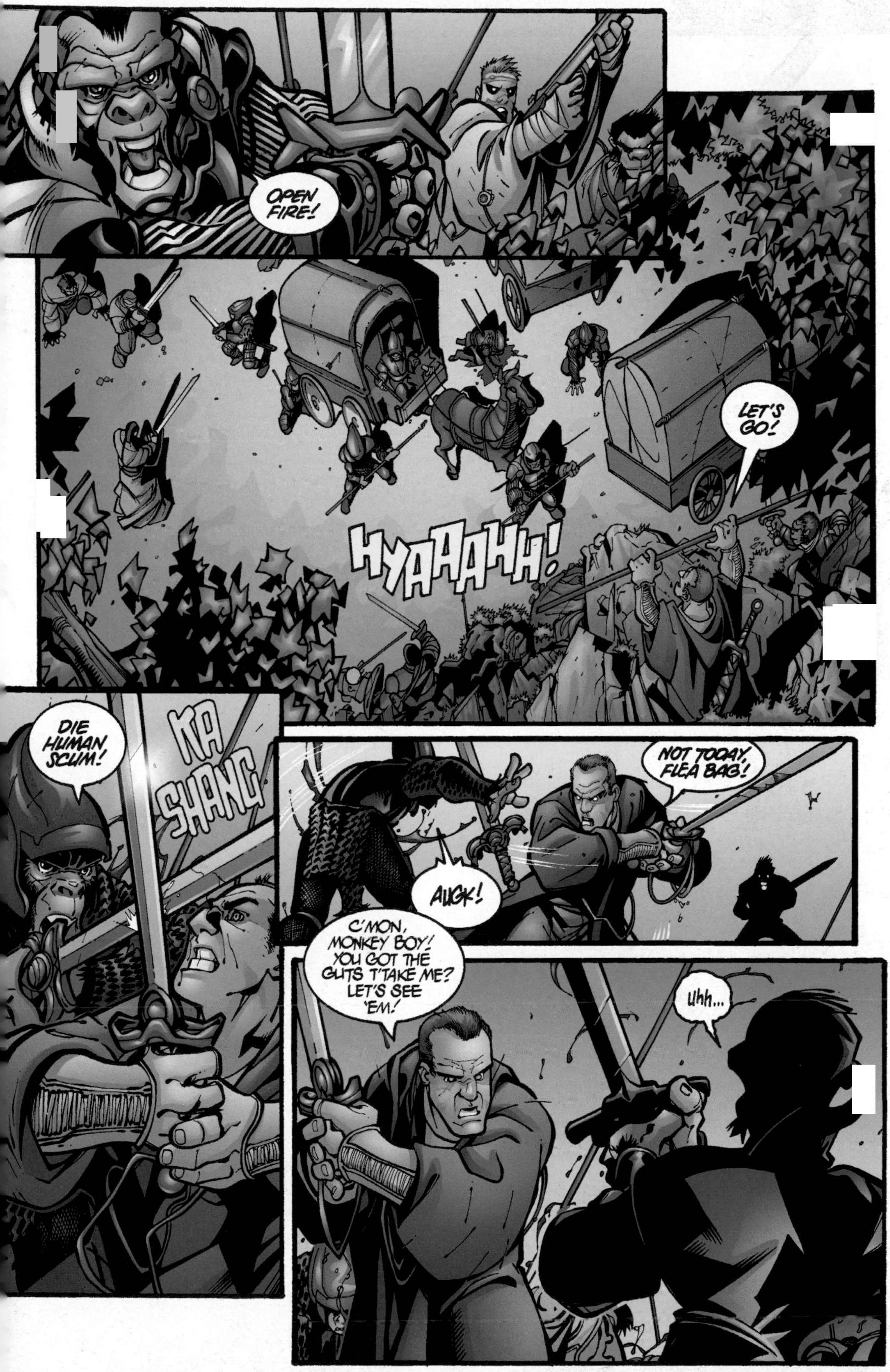
OPEN FIRE!
LET'S GO!
HYAAAHH!
DIE HUMAN SCUM!
KA SHANG
NOT TODAY, FLEA BAG!
AUGK!
C'MON, MONKEY BOY! YOU GOT THE GUTS T'TAKE ME? LET'S SEE 'EM!
Uhh...

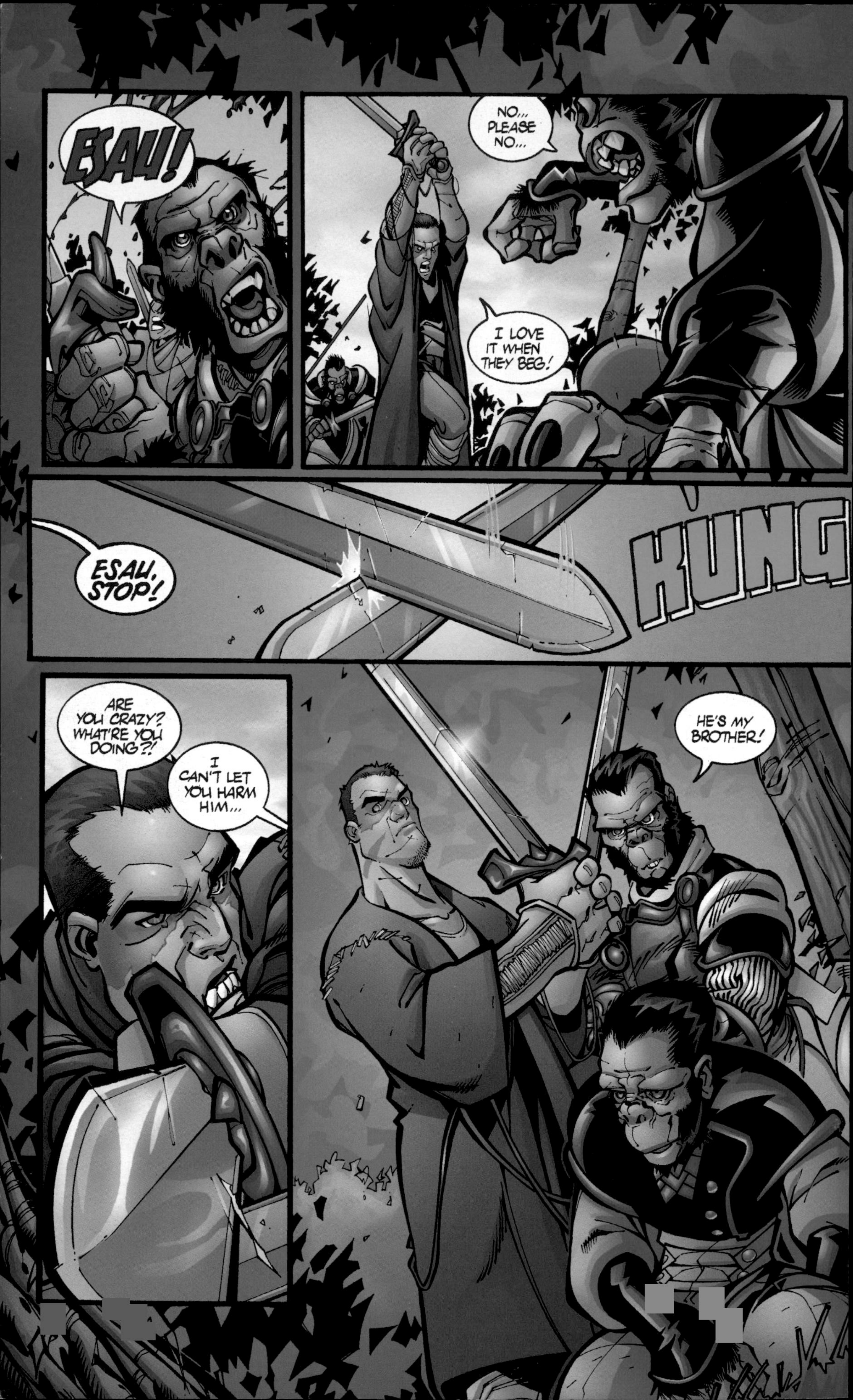
ESAU!
NO... PLEASE NO...
I LOVE IT WHEN THEY BEG!
ESAU, STOP!
KUNG
ARE YOU CRAZY? WHAT'RE YOU DOING?!
I CAN'T LET YOU HARM HIM...
HE'S MY BROTHER!

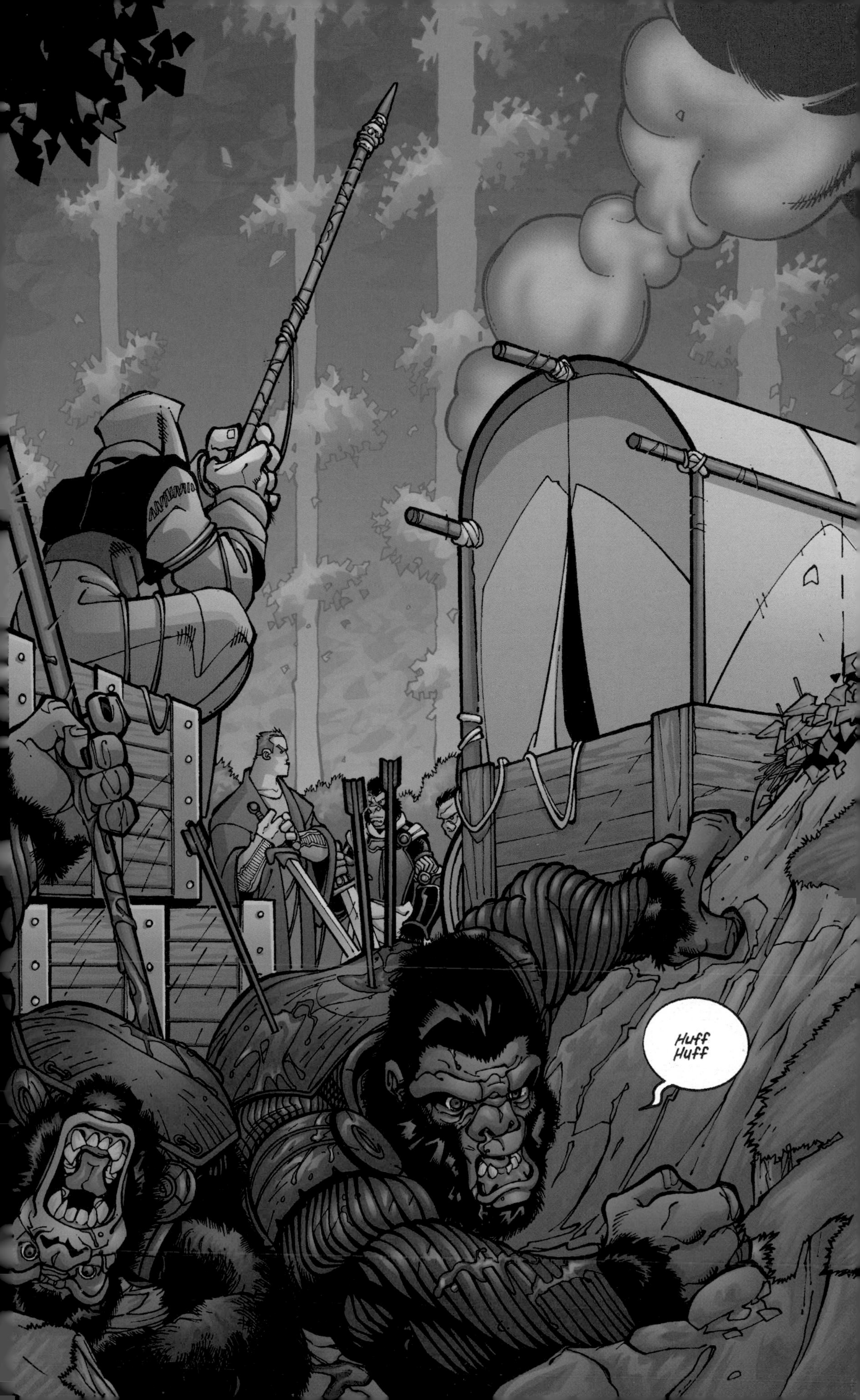
Huff Huff

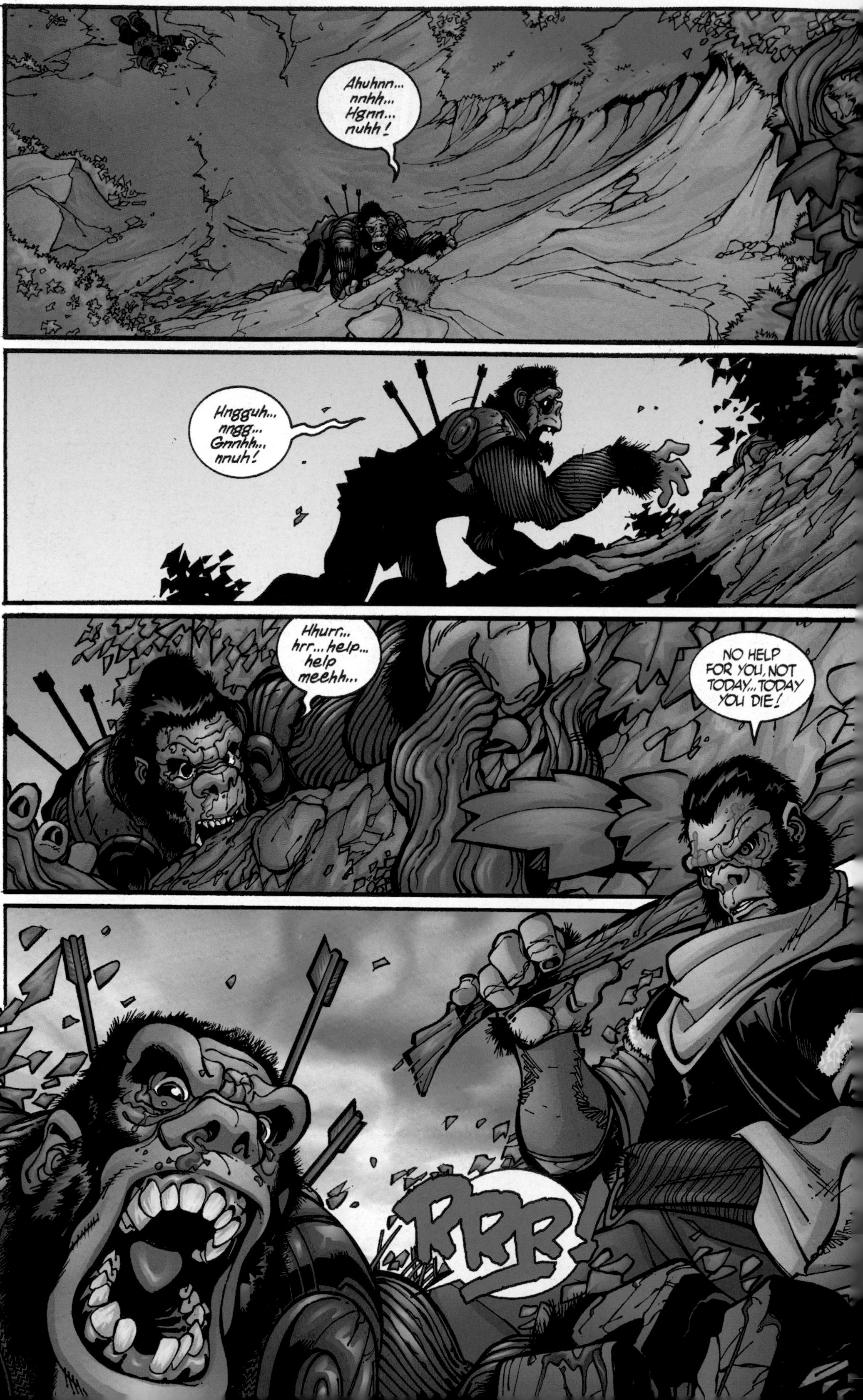
Ahuhnn... nnhh... Hgnn... nuhh!
Hngguh... nngg... Gnnhh... nnuh!
Hhurr... hrr... help... help meehh...
NO HELP FOR YOU, NOT TODAY... TODAY YOU DIE!
RRR

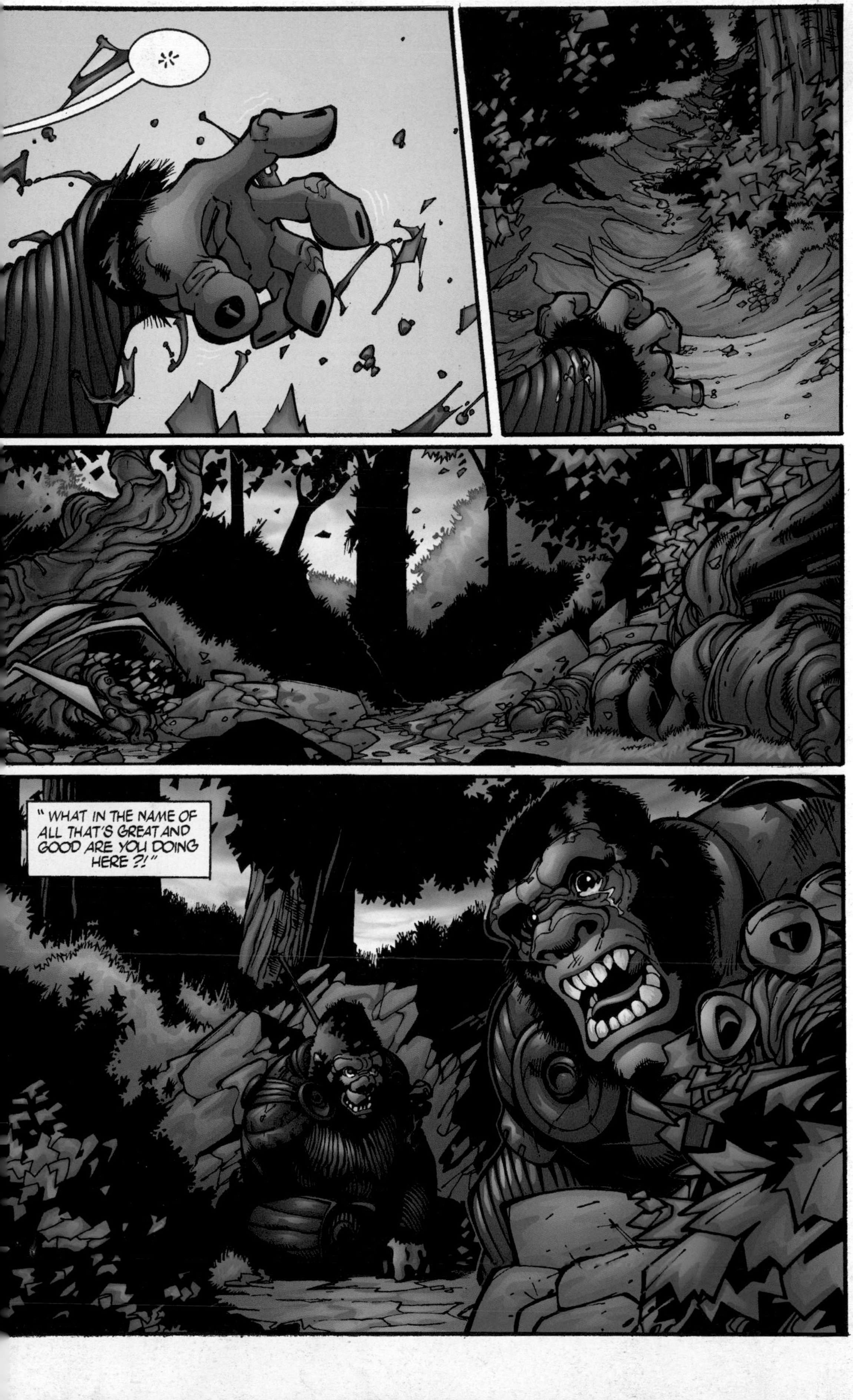
"WHAT IN THE NAME OF ALL THAT'S GREAT AND GOOD ARE YOU DOING HERE ?!"

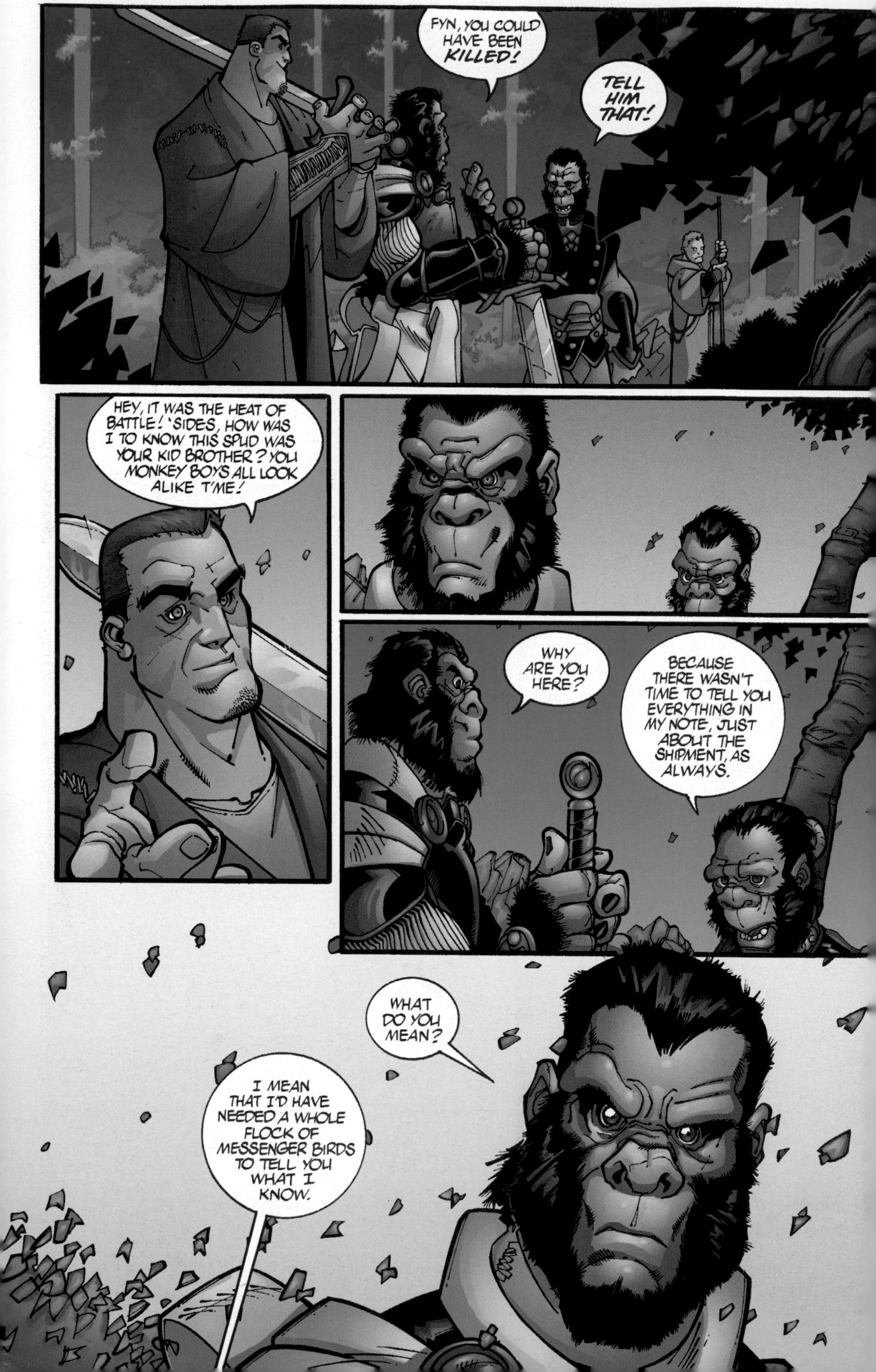
FYN, YOU COULD HAVE BEEN KILLED!
TELL HIM THAT!
HEY, IT WAS THE HEAT OF BATTLE! 'SIDES, HOW WAS I TO KNOW THIS SPUD WAS YOUR KID BROTHER? YOU MONKEY BOYS ALL LOOK ALIKE T'ME!
WHY ARE YOU HERE?
BECAUSE THERE WASN'T TIME TO TELL YOU EVERYTHING IN MY NOTE, JUST ABOUT THE SHIPMENT, AS ALWAYS.
WHAT DO YOU MEAN?
I MEAN THAT I'D HAVE NEEDED A WHOLE FLOCK OF MESSENGER BIRDS TO TELL YOU WHAT I KNOW.

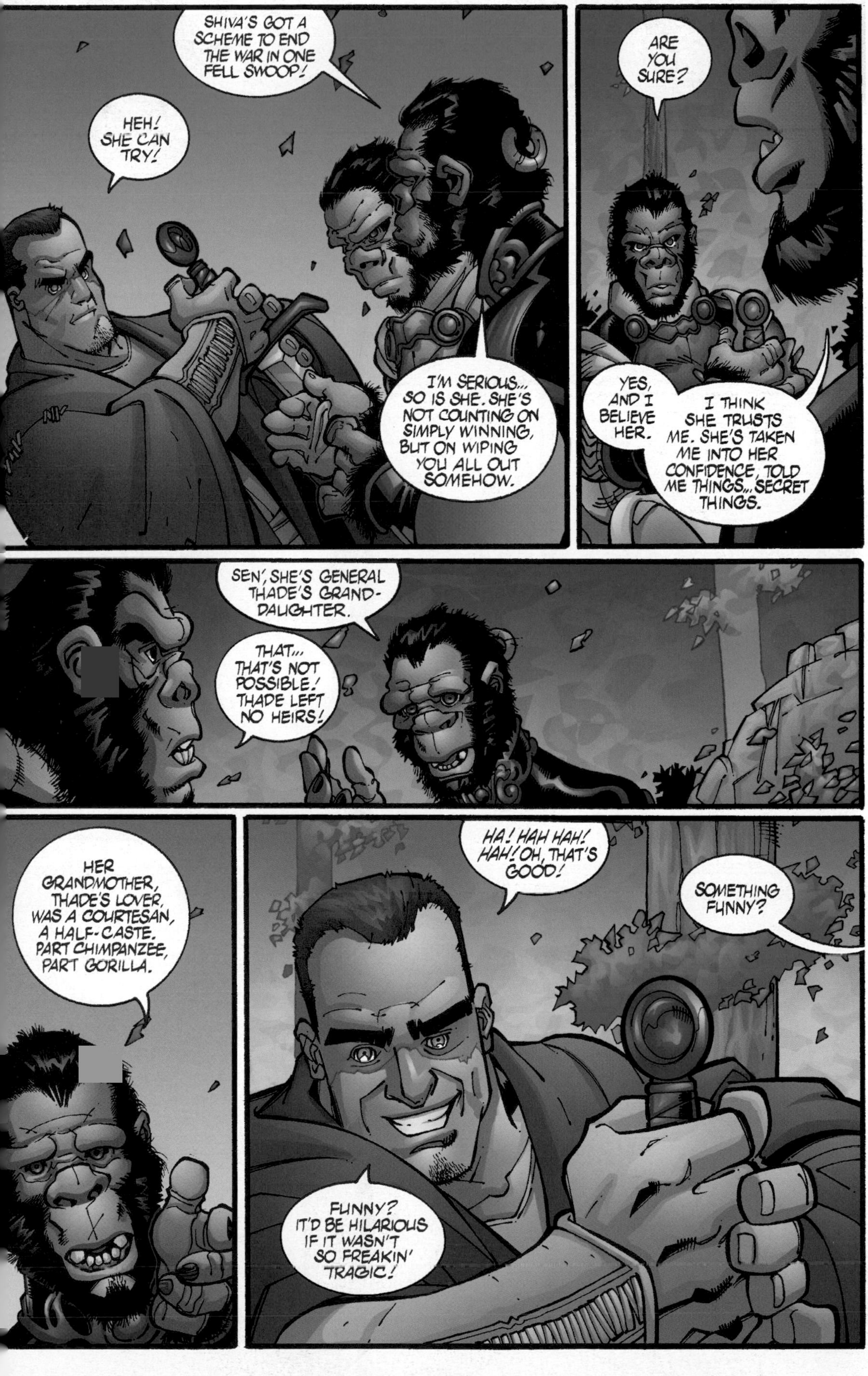
SHIVA'S GOT A SCHEME TO END THE WAR IN ONE FELL SWOOP!
HEH! SHE CAN TRY!
I'M SERIOUS... SO IS SHE. SHE'S NOT COUNTING ON SIMPLY WINNING, BUT ON WIPING YOU ALL OUT SOMEHOW.
ARE YOU SURE?
YES, AND I BELIEVE HER.
I THINK SHE TRUSTS ME. SHE'S TAKEN ME INTO HER CONFIDENCE, TOLD ME THINGS... SECRET THINGS.
SEN, SHE'S GENERAL THADE'S GRAND-DAUGHTER.
THAT... THAT'S NOT POSSIBLE! THADE LEFT NO HEIRS!
HER GRANDMOTHER, THADE'S LOVER, WAS A COURTESAN, A HALF-CASTE. PART CHIMPANZEE, PART GORILLA.
HA! HAH HAH! HAH! OH, THAT'S GOOD!
SOMETHING FUNNY?
FUNNY? IT'D BE HILARIOUS IF IT WASN'T SO FREAKIN' TRAGIC!

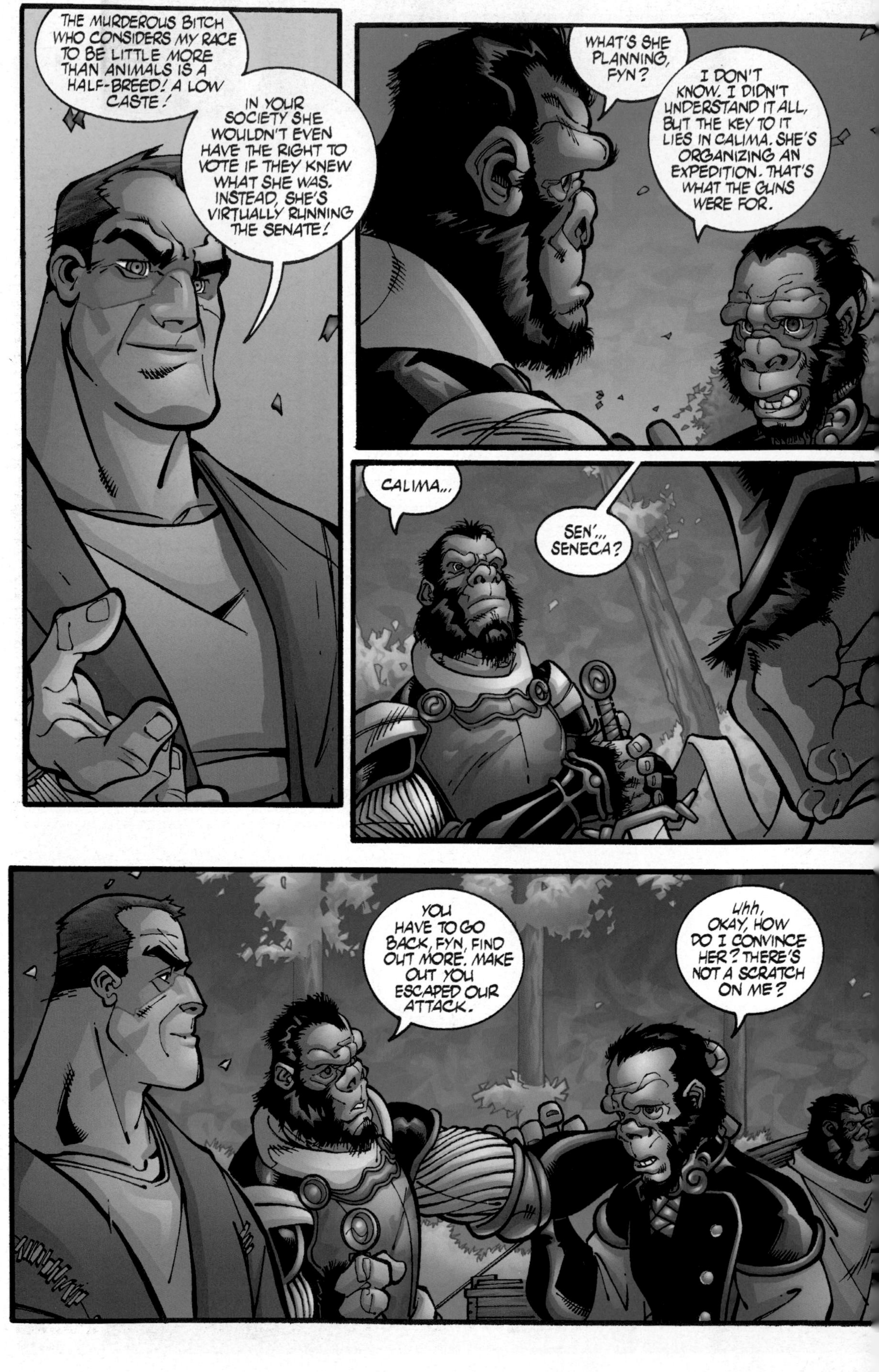
THE MURDEROUS BITCH WHO CONSIDERS MY RACE TO BE LITTLE MORE THAN ANIMALS IS A HALF-BREED! A LOW CASTE!
IN YOUR SOCIETY SHE WOULDN'T EVEN HAVE THE RIGHT TO VOTE IF THEY KNEW WHAT SHE WAS. INSTEAD, SHE'S VIRTUALLY RUNNING THE SENATE!
WHAT'S SHE PLANNING, FYN?
I DON'T KNOW. I DIDN'T UNDERSTAND IT ALL, BUT THE KEY TO IT LIES IN CALIMA. SHE'S ORGANIZING AN EXPEDITION. THAT'S WHAT THE GUNS WERE FOR.
CALIMA...
SEN'... SENECA?
YOU HAVE TO GO BACK, FYN, FIND OUT MORE. MAKE OUT YOU ESCAPED OUR ATTACK.
UHH, OKAY, HOW DO I CONVINCE HER? THERE'S NOT A SCRATCH ON ME?

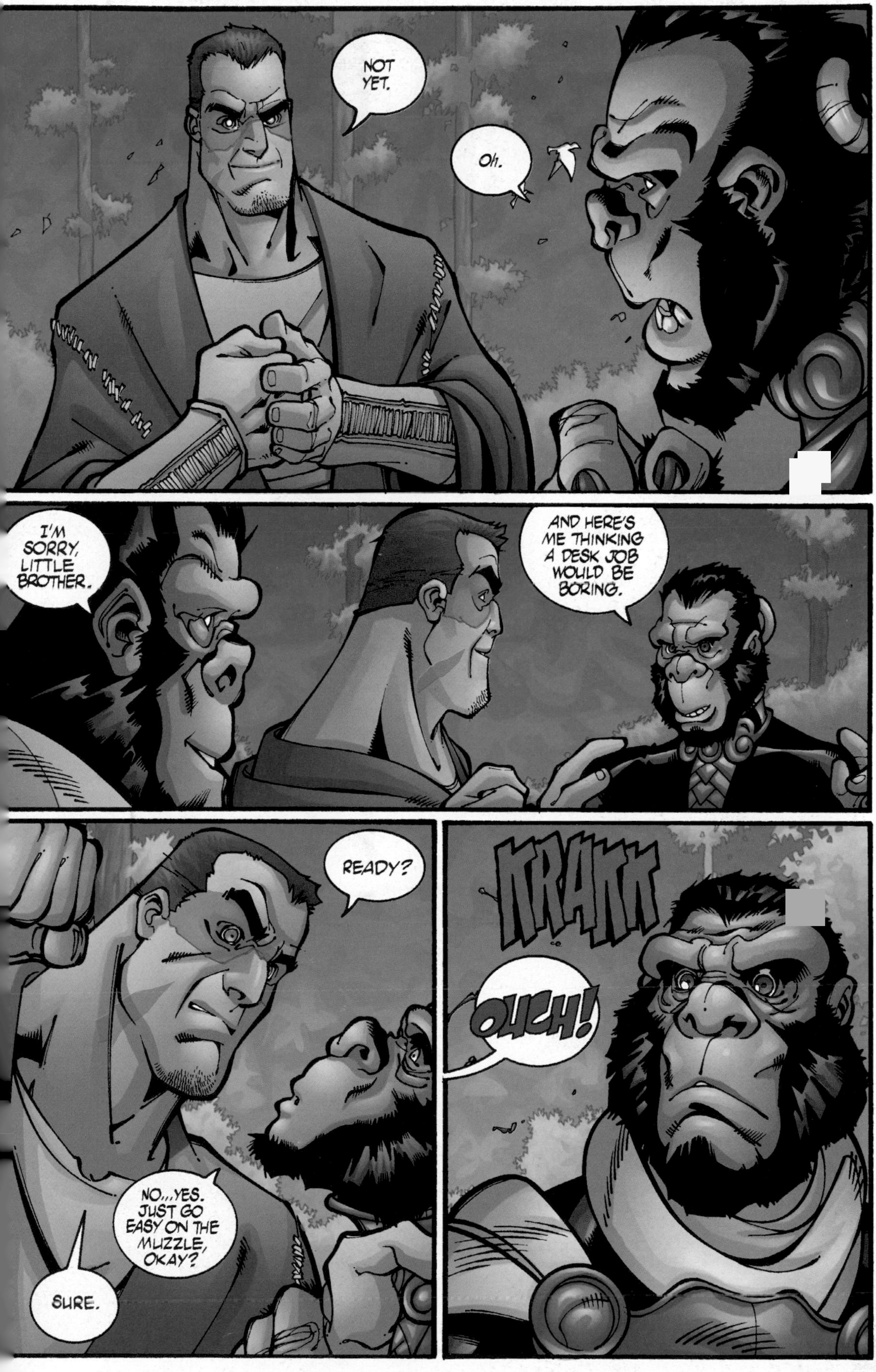
NOT YET.
OH.
I'M SORRY, LITTLE BROTHER.
AND HERE'S ME THINKING A DESK JOB WOULD BE BORING.
READY?
NO... YES. JUST GO EASY ON THE MUZZLE, OKAY?
SURE.
KRAKK
OUCH!

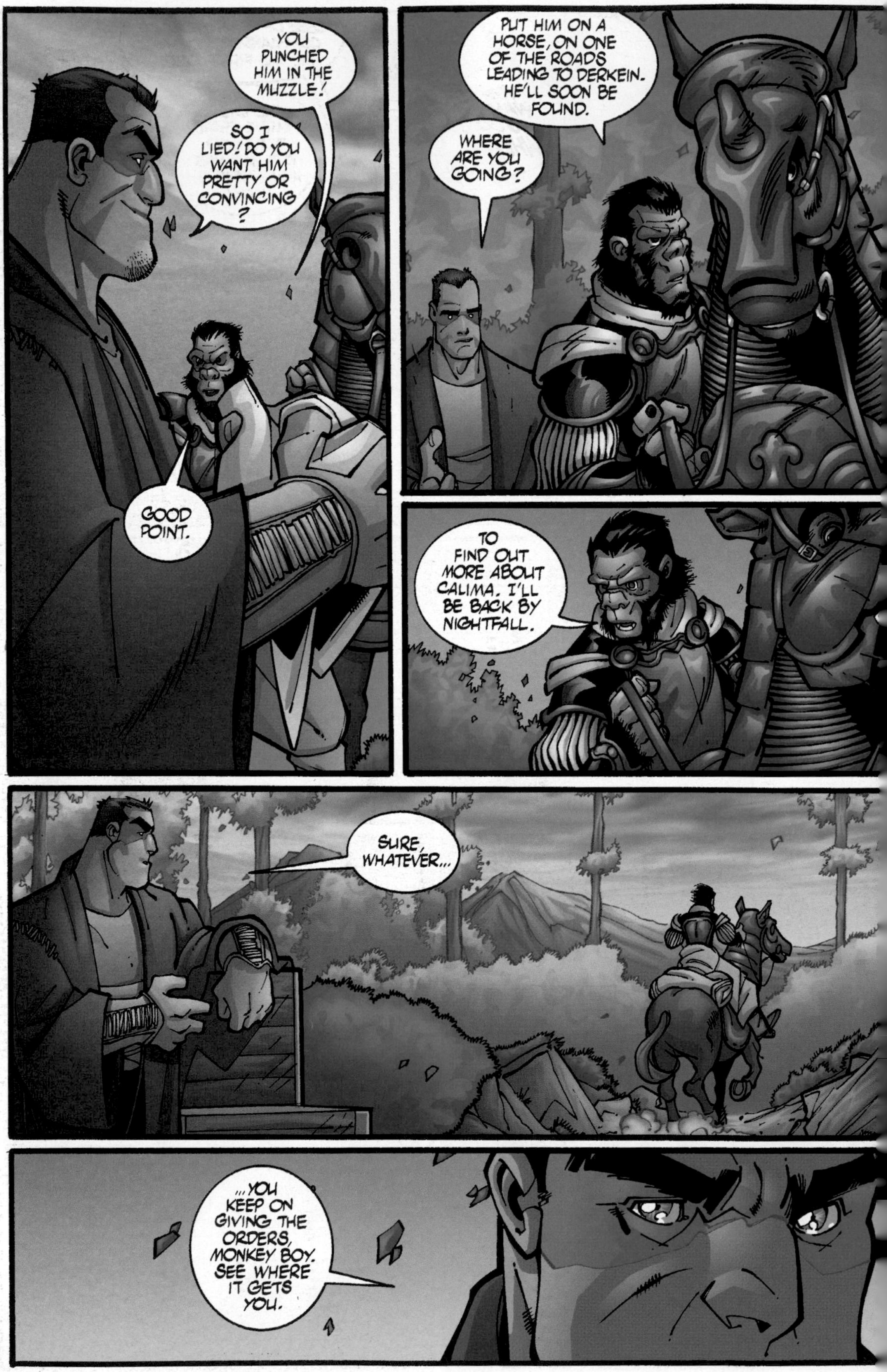
YOU PUNCHED HIM IN THE MUZZLE!
SO I LIED! DO YOU WANT HIM PRETTY OR CONVINCING?
GOOD POINT.
PUT HIM ON A HORSE, ON ONE OF THE ROADS LEADING TO DERKEIN. HE'LL SOON BE FOUND.
WHERE ARE YOU GOING?
TO FIND OUT MORE ABOUT CALIMA. I'LL BE BACK BY NIGHTFALL.
SURE, WHATEVER...
...YOU KEEP ON GIVING THE ORDERS, MONKEY BOY. SEE WHERE IT GETS YOU.

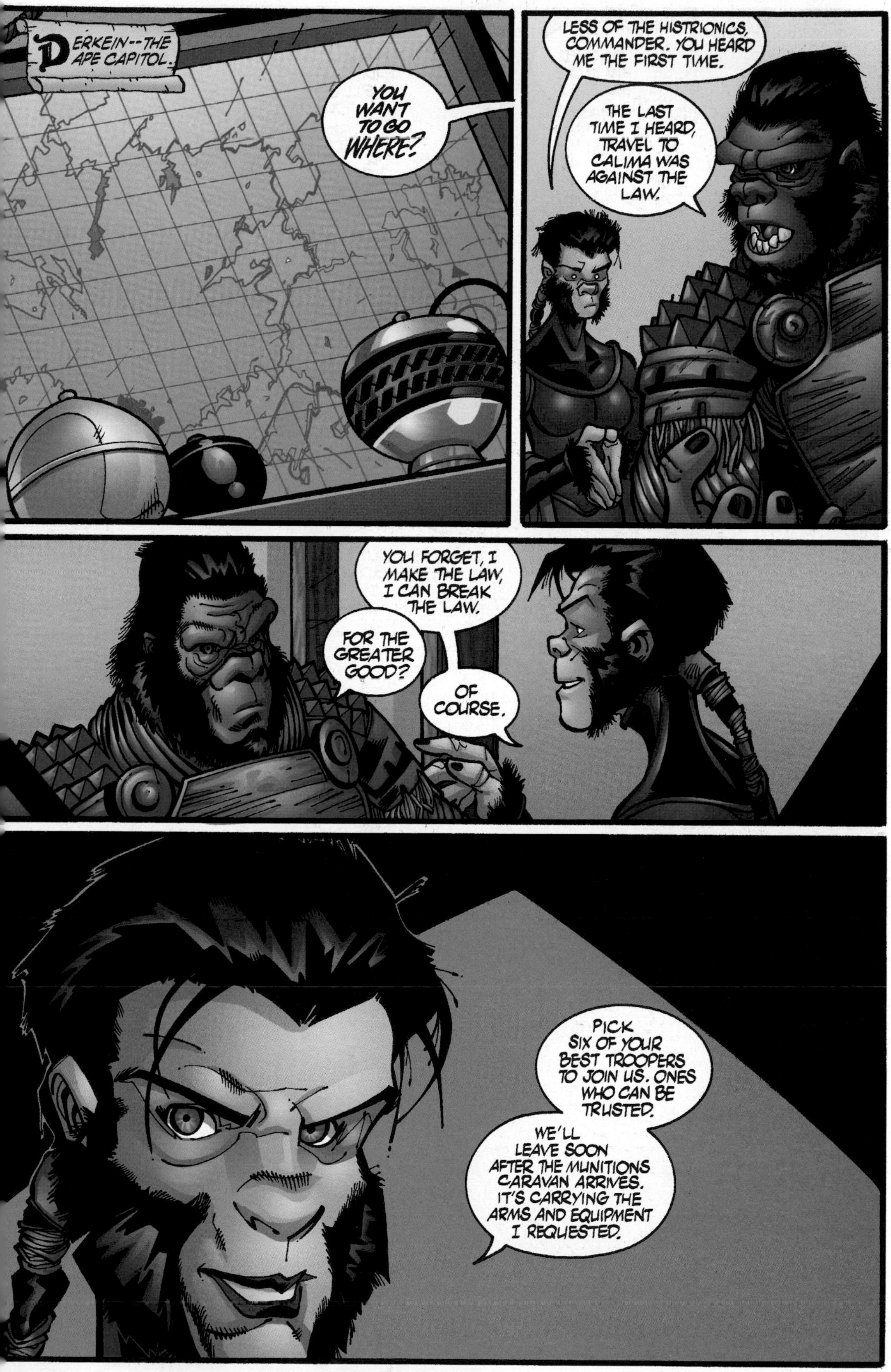
DERKEIN--THE APE CAPITOL.
YOU WANT TO GO WHERE?
LESS OF THE HISTRIONICS, COMMANDER. YOU HEARD ME THE FIRST TIME.
THE LAST TIME I HEARD, TRAVEL TO CALIMA WAS AGAINST THE LAW.
YOU FORGET, I MAKE THE LAW, I CAN BREAK THE LAW.
FOR THE GREATER GOOD?
OF COURSE.
PICK SIX OF YOUR BEST TROOPERS TO JOIN US. ONES WHO CAN BE TRUSTED.
WE'LL LEAVE SOON AFTER THE MUNITIONS CARAVAN ARRIVES. IT'S CARRYING THE ARMS AND EQUIPMENT I REQUESTED.

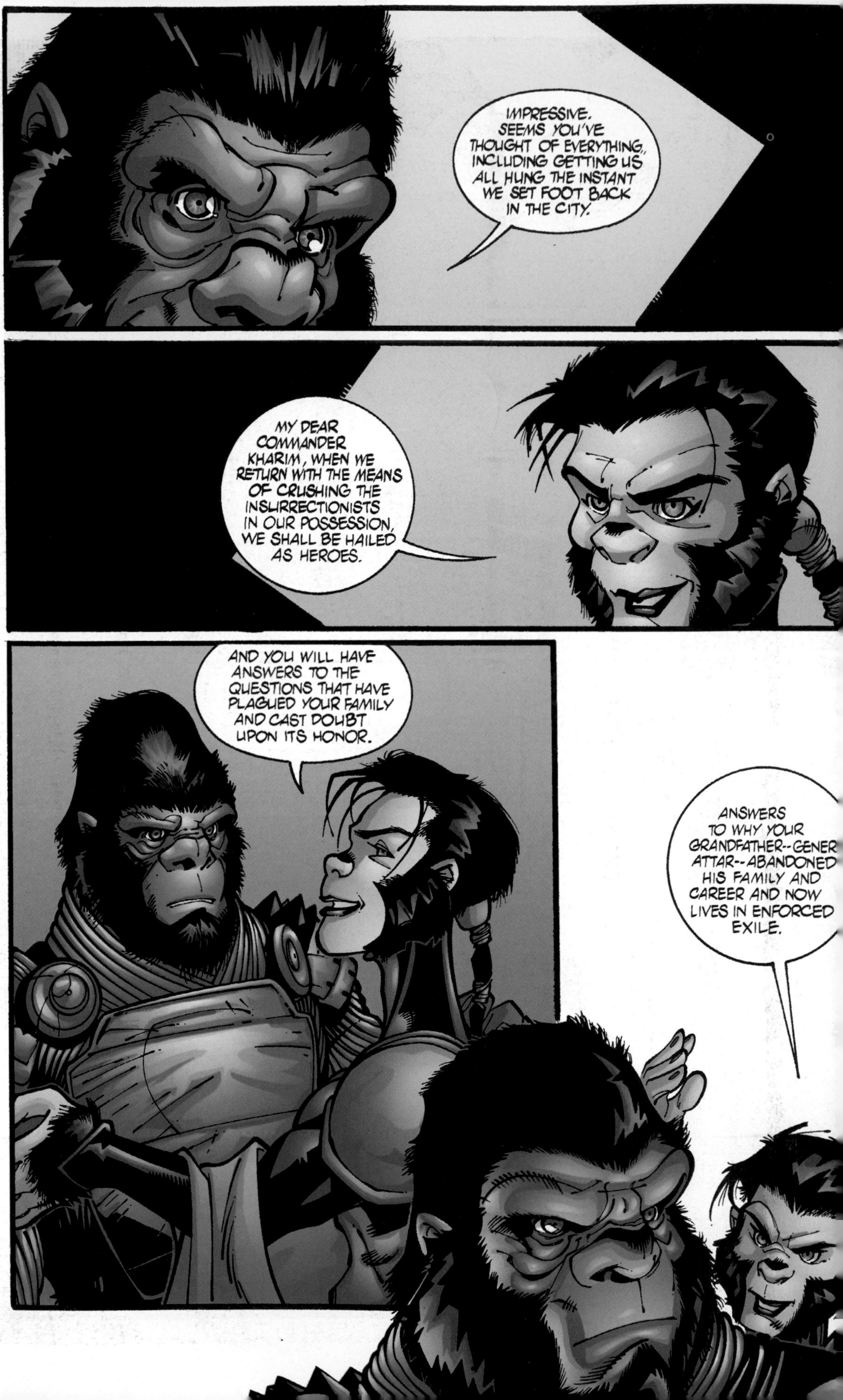
IMPRESSIVE. SEEMS YOU'VE THOUGHT OF EVERYTHING, INCLUDING GETTING US ALL HUNG THE INSTANT WE SET FOOT BACK IN THE CITY.
MY DEAR COMMANDER KHARIM, WHEN WE RETURN WITH THE MEANS OF CRUSHING THE INSURRECTIONISTS IN OUR POSSESSION, WE SHALL BE HAILED AS HEROES.
AND YOU WILL HAVE ANSWERS TO THE QUESTIONS THAT HAVE PLAGUED YOUR FAMILY AND CAST DOUBT UPON ITS HONOR.
ANSWERS TO WHY YOUR GRANDFATHER--GENER ATTAR--ABANDONED HIS FAMILY AND CAREER AND NOW LIVES IN ENFORCED EXILE.

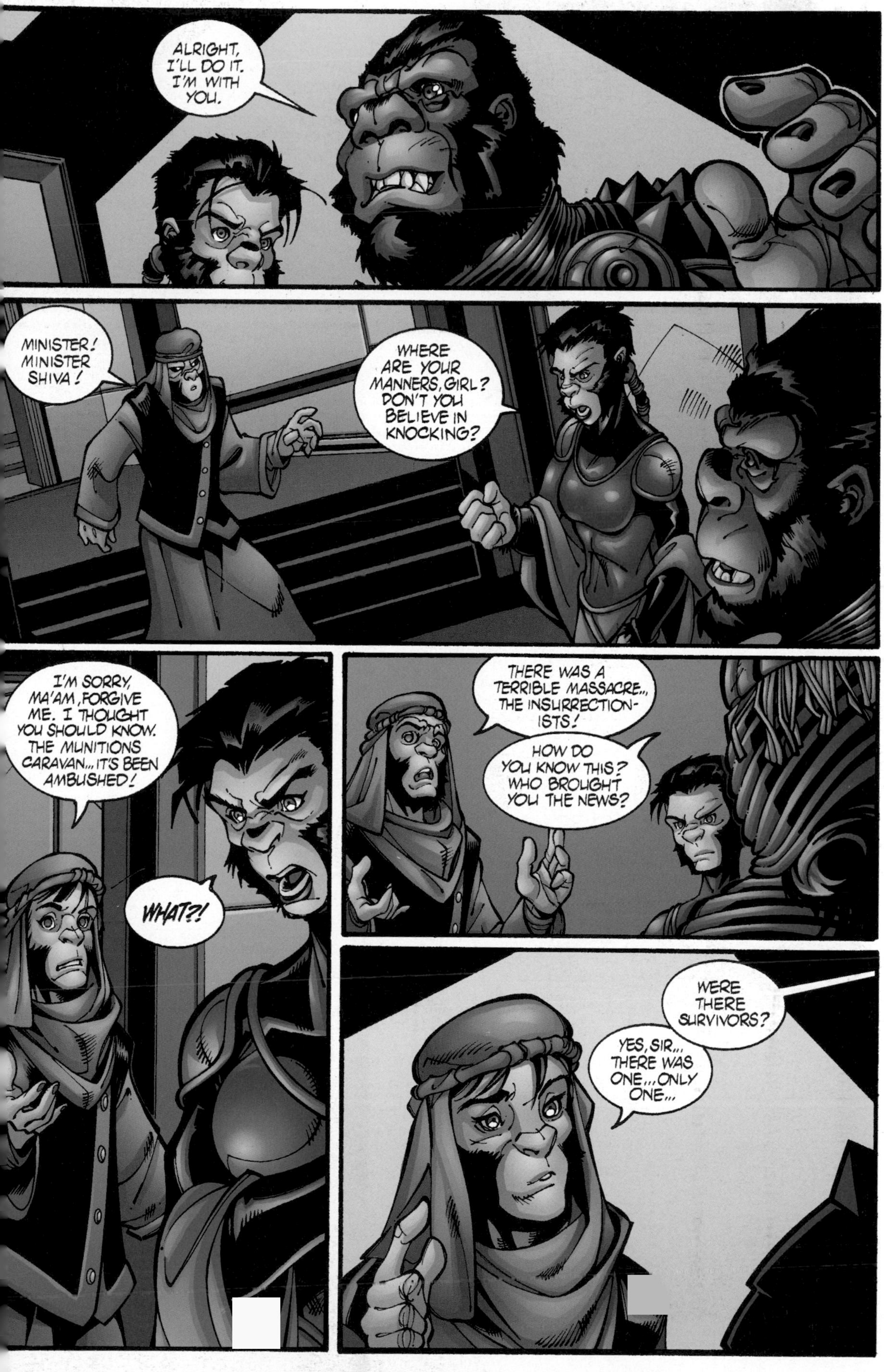
ALRIGHT, I'LL DO IT. I'M WITH YOU.
MINISTER! MINISTER SHIVA!
WHERE ARE YOUR MANNERS, GIRL? DON'T YOU BELIEVE IN KNOCKING?
I'M SORRY, MA'AM, FORGIVE ME. I THOUGHT YOU SHOULD KNOW. THE MUNITIONS CARAVAN... IT'S BEEN AMBUSHED!
WHAT?!
THERE WAS A TERRIBLE MASSACRE... THE INSURRECTIONISTS!
HOW DO YOU KNOW THIS? WHO BROUGHT YOU THE NEWS?
WERE THERE SURVIVORS?
YES, SIR... THERE WAS ONE... ONLY ONE...

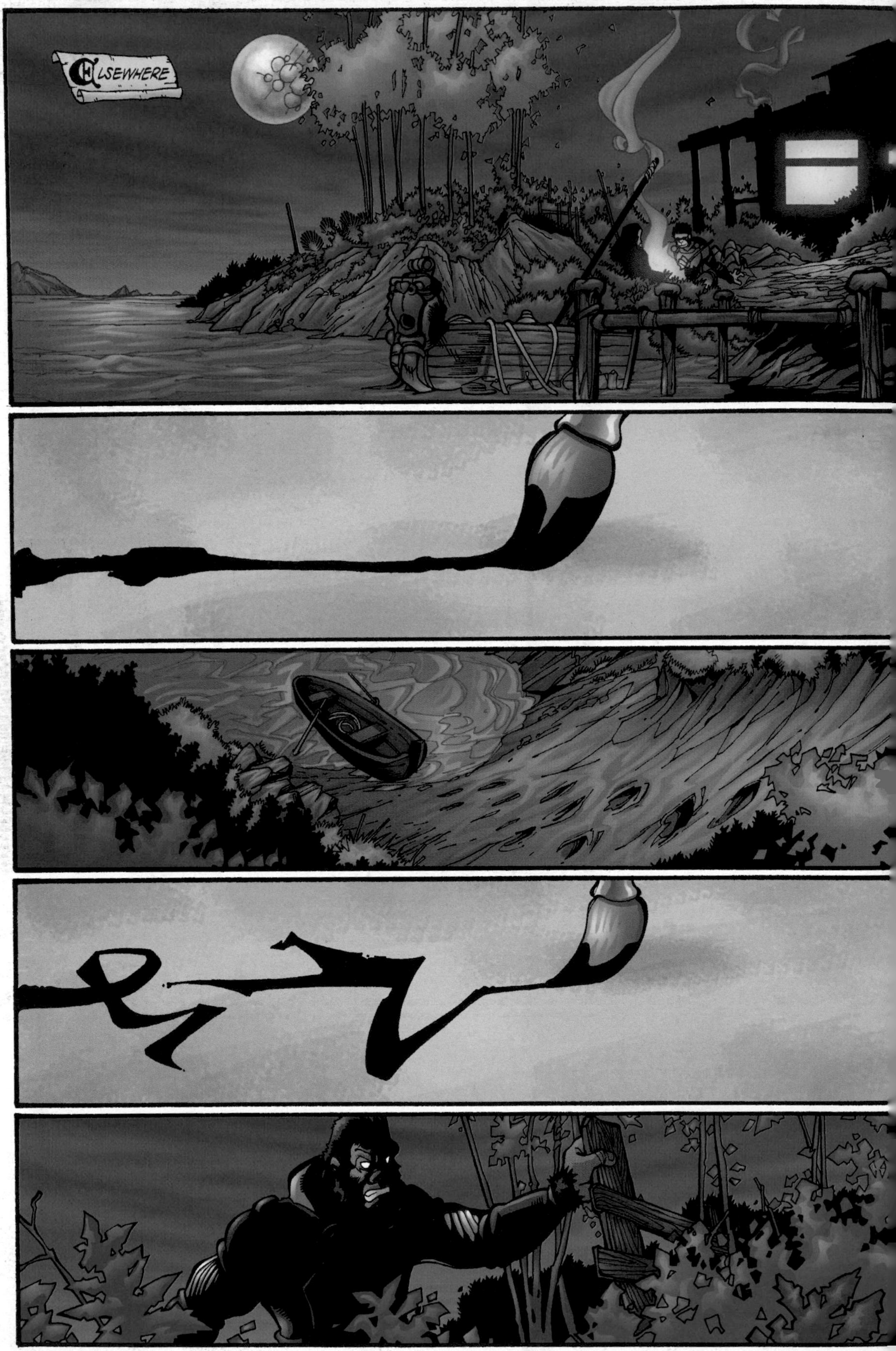
ELSEWHERE

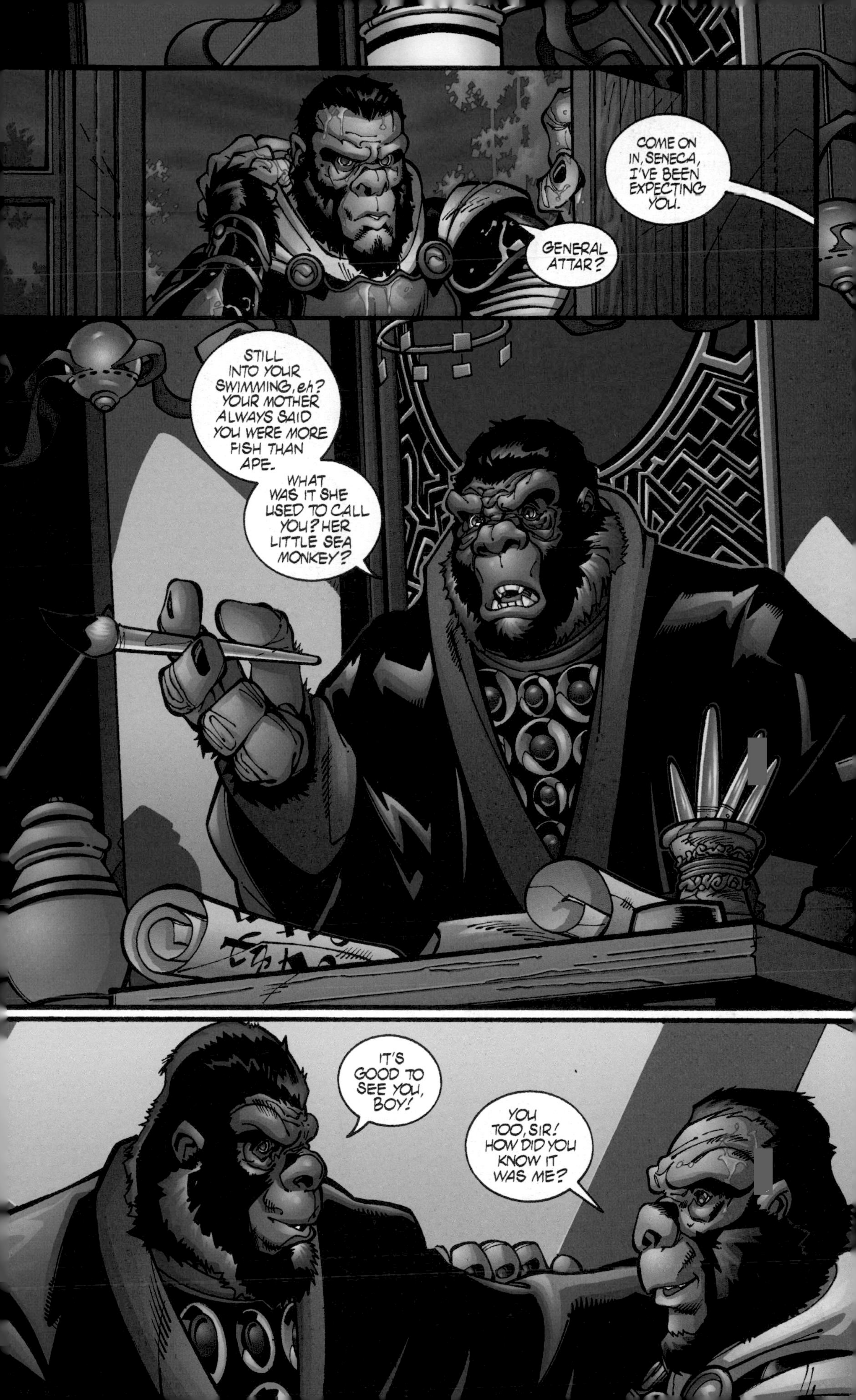
GENERAL ATTAR?
COME ON IN, SENECA, I'VE BEEN EXPECTING YOU.
STILL INTO YOUR SWIMMING, eh? YOUR MOTHER ALWAYS SAID YOU WERE MORE FISH THAN APE.
WHAT WAS IT SHE USED TO CALL YOU? HER LITTLE SEA MONKEY?
IT'S GOOD TO SEE YOU, BOY!
YOU TOO, SIR! HOW DID YOU KNOW IT WAS ME?

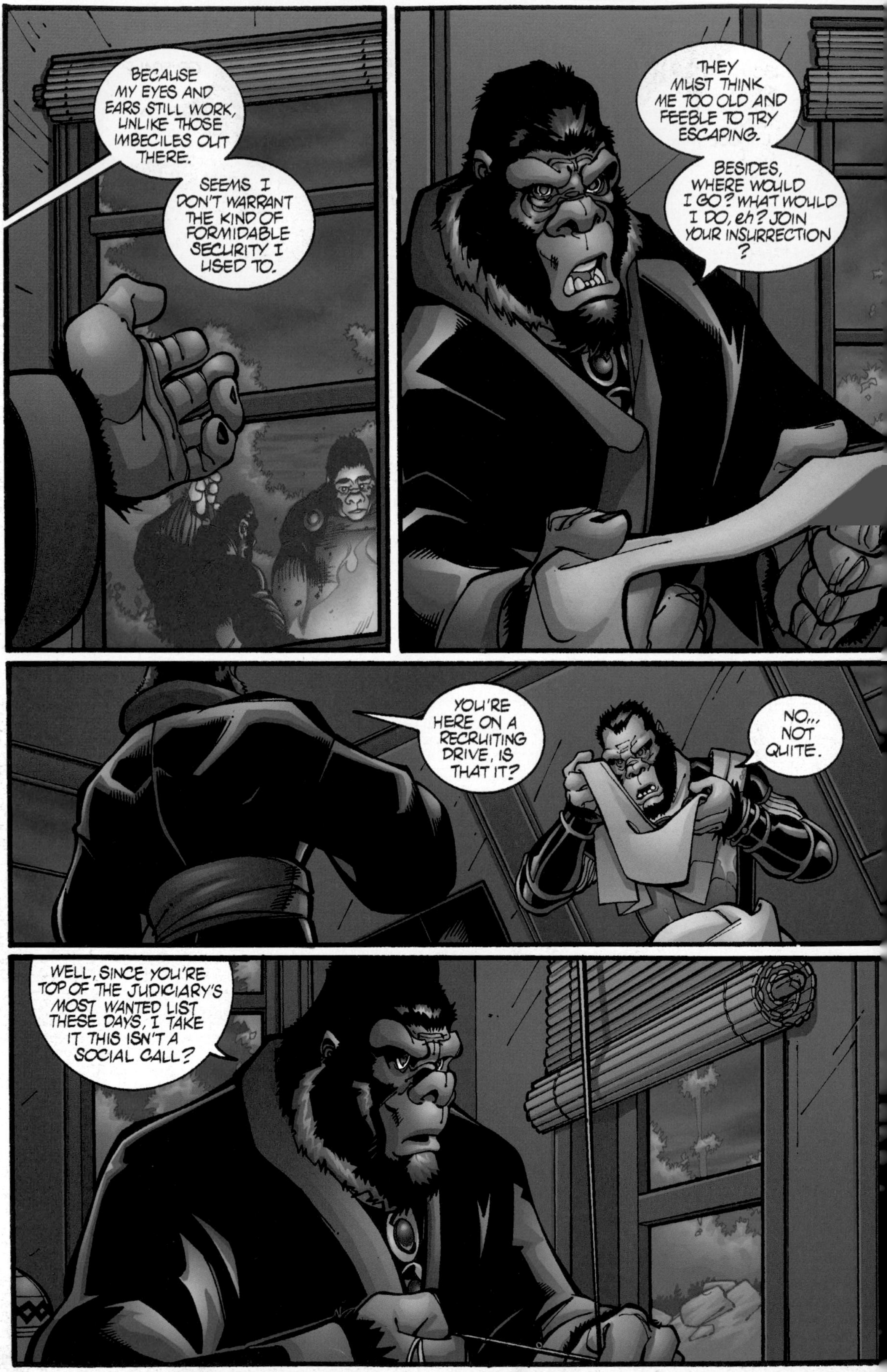
BECAUSE MY EYES AND EARS STILL WORK, UNLIKE THOSE IMBECILES OUT THERE.
SEEMS I DON'T WARRANT THE KIND OF FORMIDABLE SECURITY I USED TO.
THEY MUST THINK ME TOO OLD AND FEEBLE TO TRY ESCAPING.
BESIDES, WHERE WOULD I GO? WHAT WOULD I DO, eh? JOIN YOUR INSURRECTION?
YOU'RE HERE ON A RECRUITING DRIVE, IS THAT IT?
NO... NOT QUITE.
WELL, SINCE YOU'RE TOP OF THE JUDICIARY'S MOST WANTED LIST THESE DAYS, I TAKE IT THIS ISN'T A SOCIAL CALL?

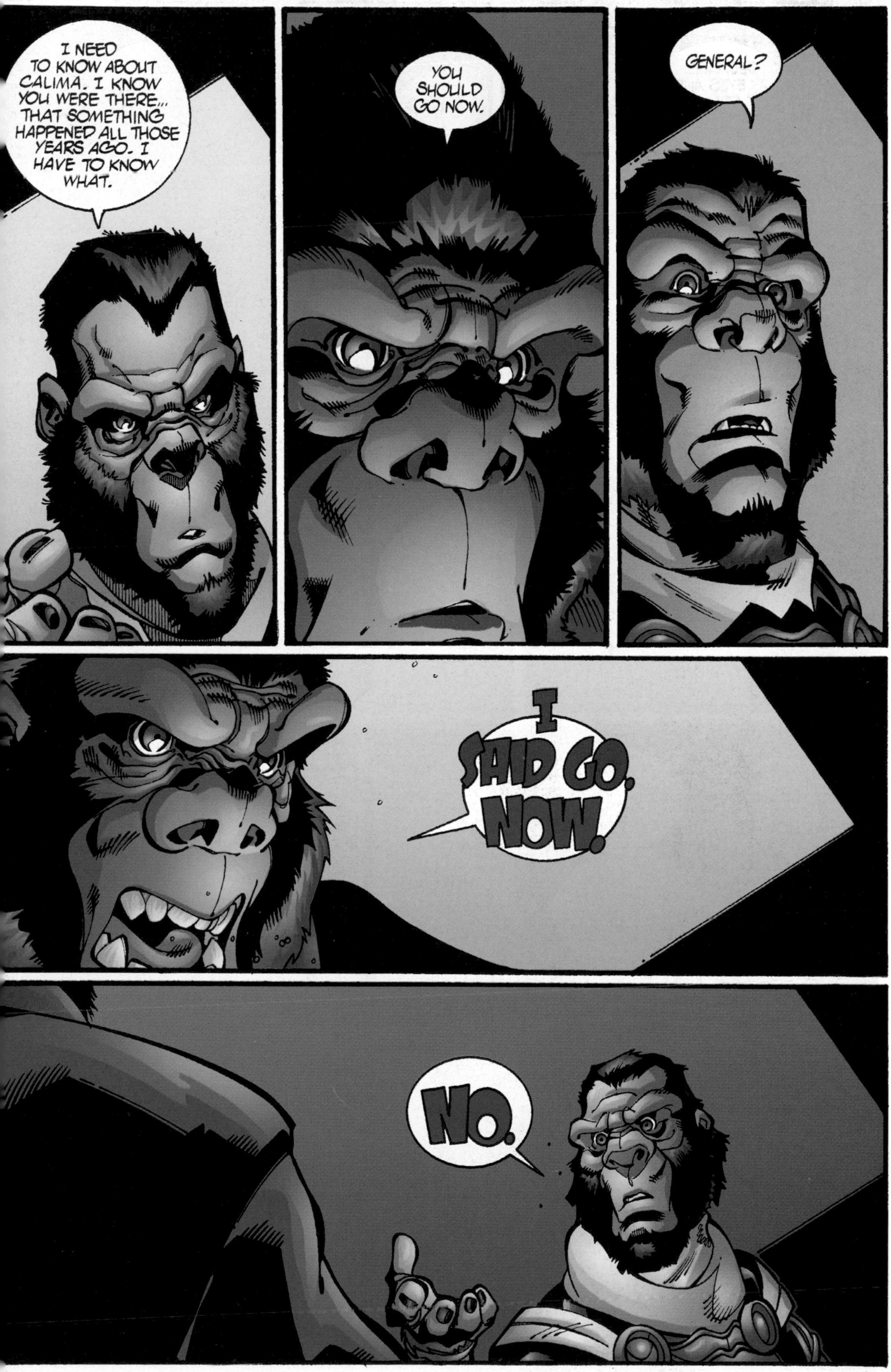
I NEED TO KNOW ABOUT CALIMA. I KNOW YOU WERE THERE... THAT SOMETHING HAPPENED ALL THOSE YEARS AGO. I HAVE TO KNOW WHAT.
YOU SHOULD GO NOW.
GENERAL?
I SAID GO. NOW.
NO.

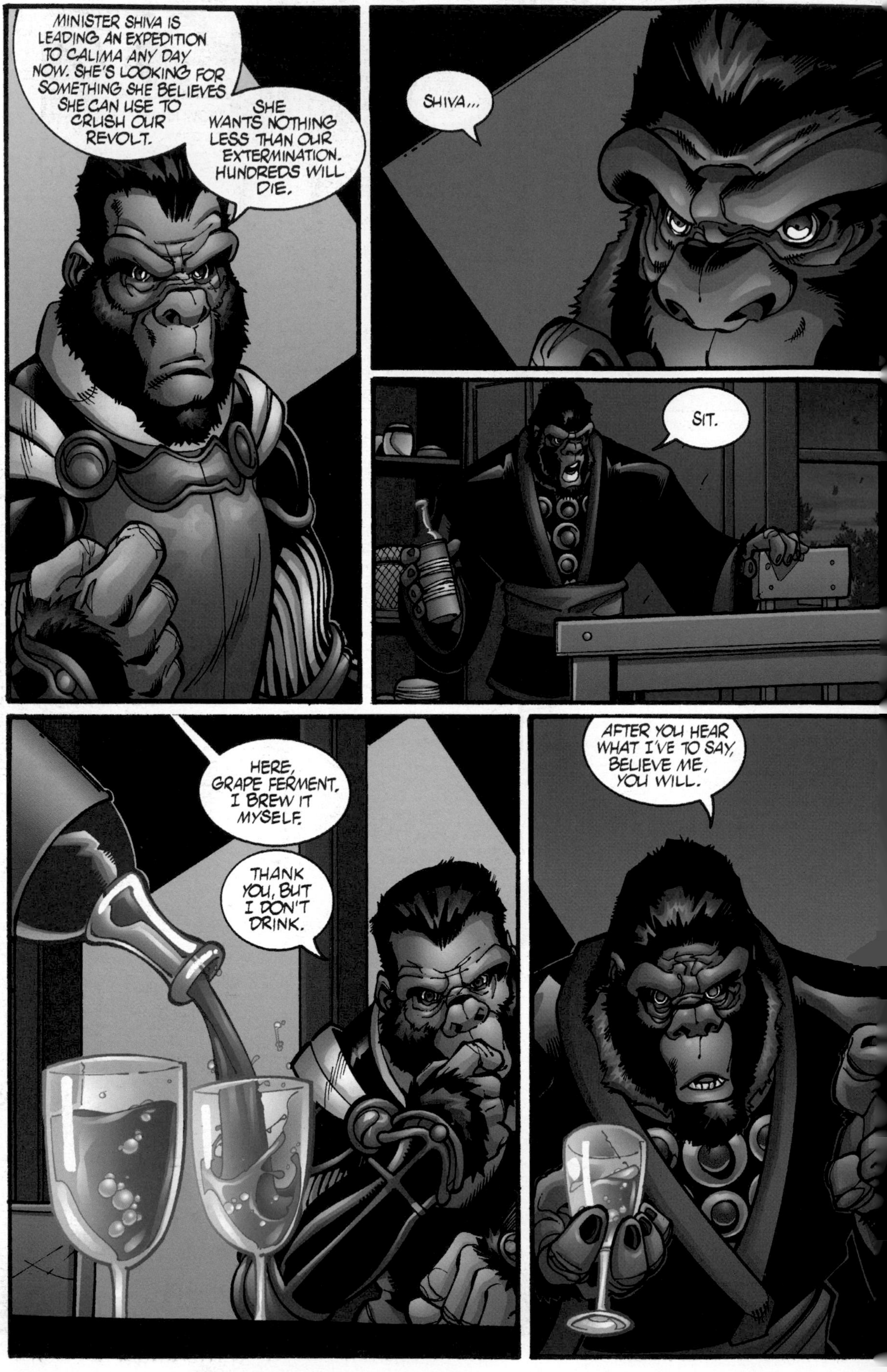
MINISTER SHIVA IS LEADING AN EXPEDITION TO CALIMA ANY DAY NOW. SHE'S LOOKING FOR SOMETHING SHE BELIEVES SHE CAN USE TO CRUSH OUR REVOLT.
SHE WANTS NOTHING LESS THAN OUR EXTERMINATION. HUNDREDS WILL DIE.
SHIVA...
SIT.
HERE, GRAPE FERMENT. I BREW IT MYSELF.
THANK YOU, BUT I DON'T DRINK.
AFTER YOU HEAR WHAT I'VE TO SAY, BELIEVE ME, YOU WILL.

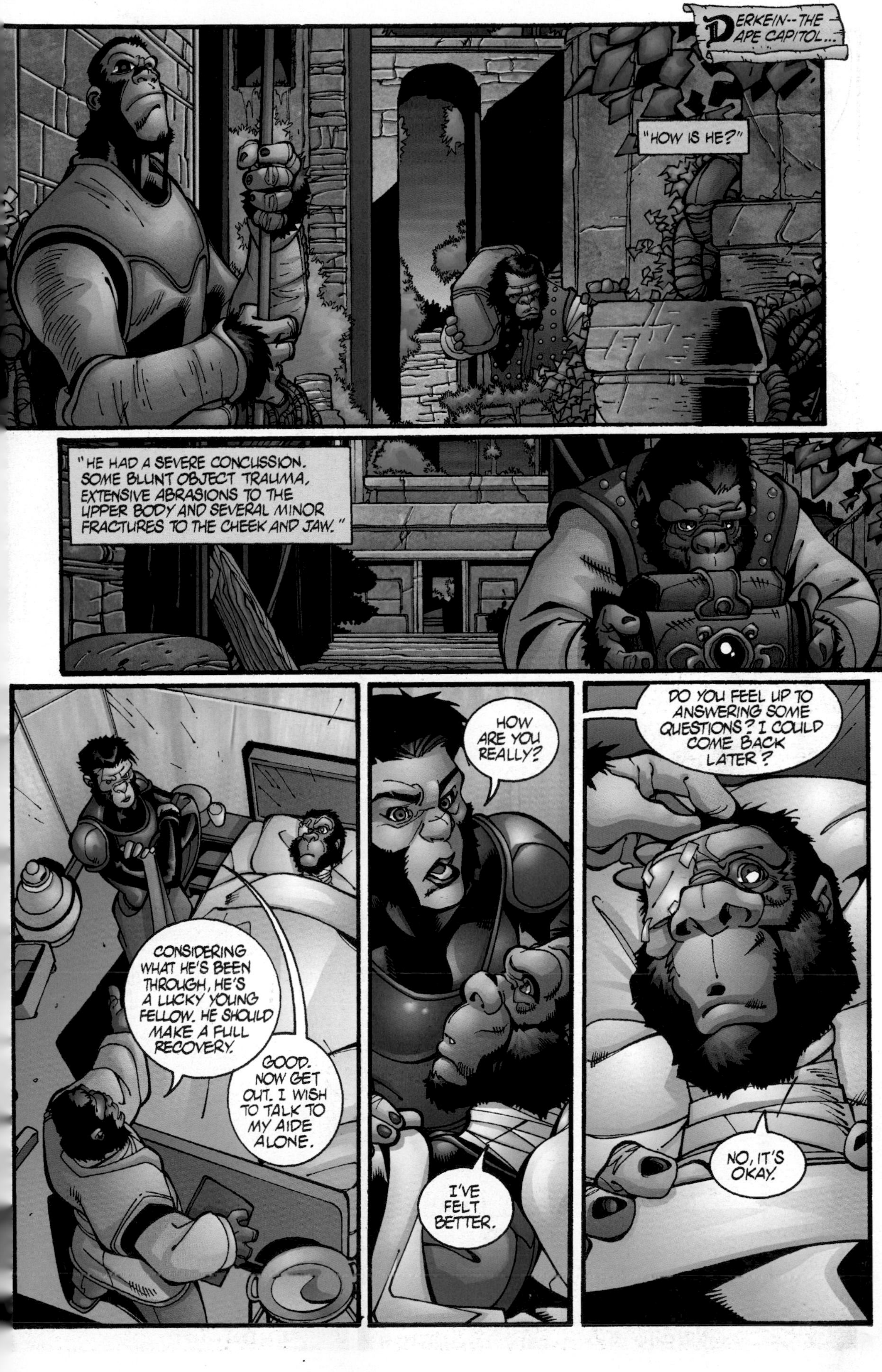
DERKEIN--THE APE CAPITOL...
"HOW IS HE?"
"HE HAD A SEVERE CONCUSSION. SOME BLUNT OBJECT TRAUMA, EXTENSIVE ABRASIONS TO THE UPPER BODY AND SEVERAL MINOR FRACTURES TO THE CHEEK AND JAW."
CONSIDERING WHAT HE'S BEEN THROUGH, HE'S A LUCKY YOUNG FELLOW. HE SHOULD MAKE A FULL RECOVERY.
GOOD. NOW GET OUT. I WISH TO TALK TO MY AIDE ALONE.
HOW ARE YOU REALLY?
I'VE FELT BETTER.
DO YOU FEEL UP TO ANSWERING SOME QUESTIONS? I COULD COME BACK LATER?
NO, IT'S OKAY.

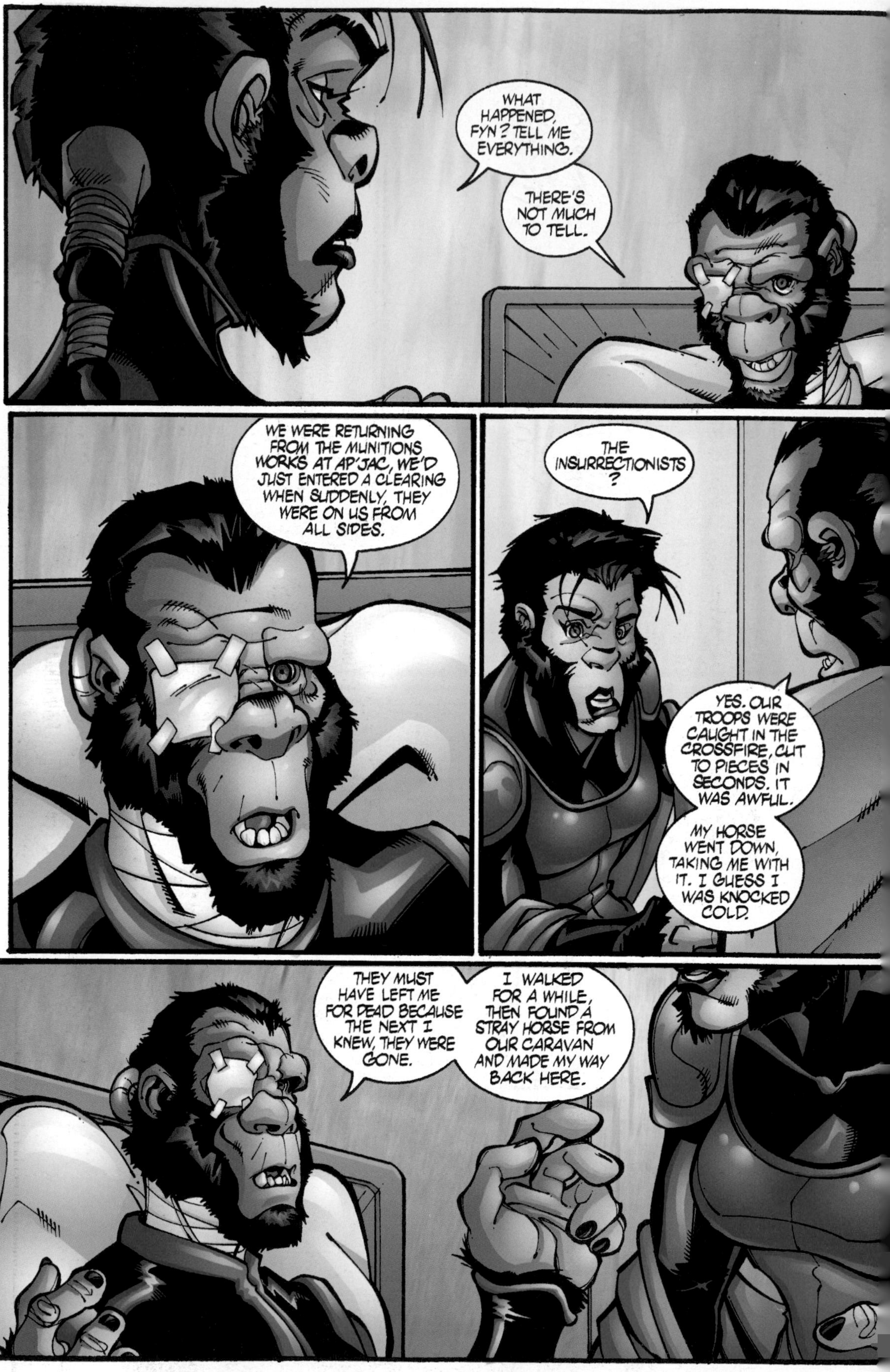
WHAT HAPPENED, FYN? TELL ME EVERYTHING.
THERE'S NOT MUCH TO TELL.
WE WERE RETURNING FROM THE MUNITIONS WORKS AT AP'JAC, WE'D JUST ENTERED A CLEARING WHEN SUDDENLY, THEY WERE ON US FROM ALL SIDES.
THE INSURRECTIONISTS?
YES. OUR TROOPS WERE CAUGHT IN THE CROSSFIRE, CUT TO PIECES IN SECONDS. IT WAS AWFUL.
MY HORSE WENT DOWN, TAKING ME WITH IT. I GUESS I WAS KNOCKED COLD.
THEY MUST HAVE LEFT ME FOR DEAD BECAUSE THE NEXT I KNEW, THEY WERE GONE.
I WALKED FOR A WHILE, THEN FOUND A STRAY HORSE FROM OUR CARAVAN AND MADE MY WAY BACK HERE.

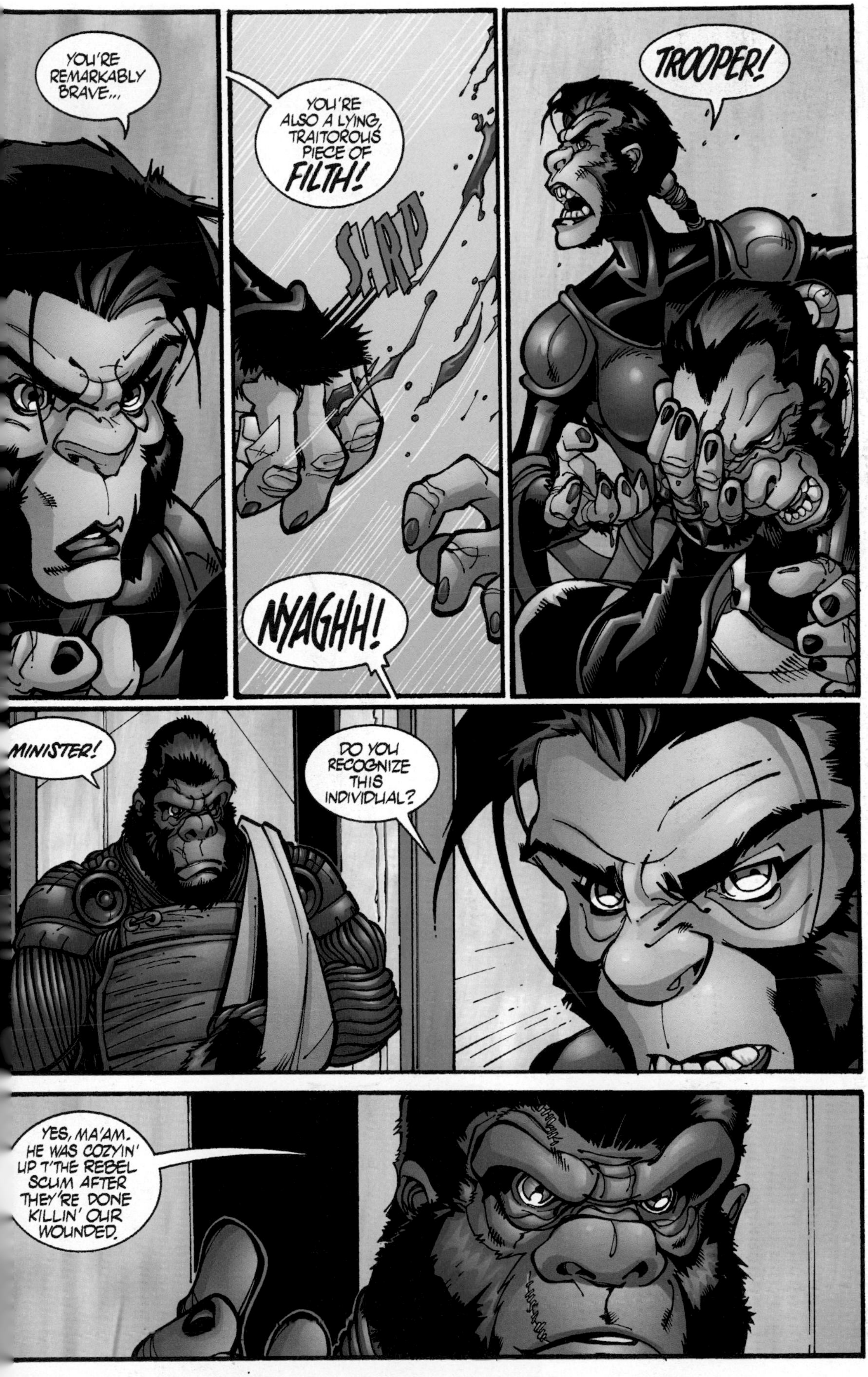
YOU'RE REMARKABLY BRAVE...
YOU'RE ALSO A LYING, TRAITOROUS PIECE OF FILTH!
SHRP
NYAGHH!
TROOPER!
MINISTER!
DO YOU RECOGNIZE THIS INDIVIDUAL?
YES, MA'AM. HE WAS COZYIN' UP T'THE REBEL SCUM AFTER THEY'RE DONE KILLIN' OUR WOUNDED.

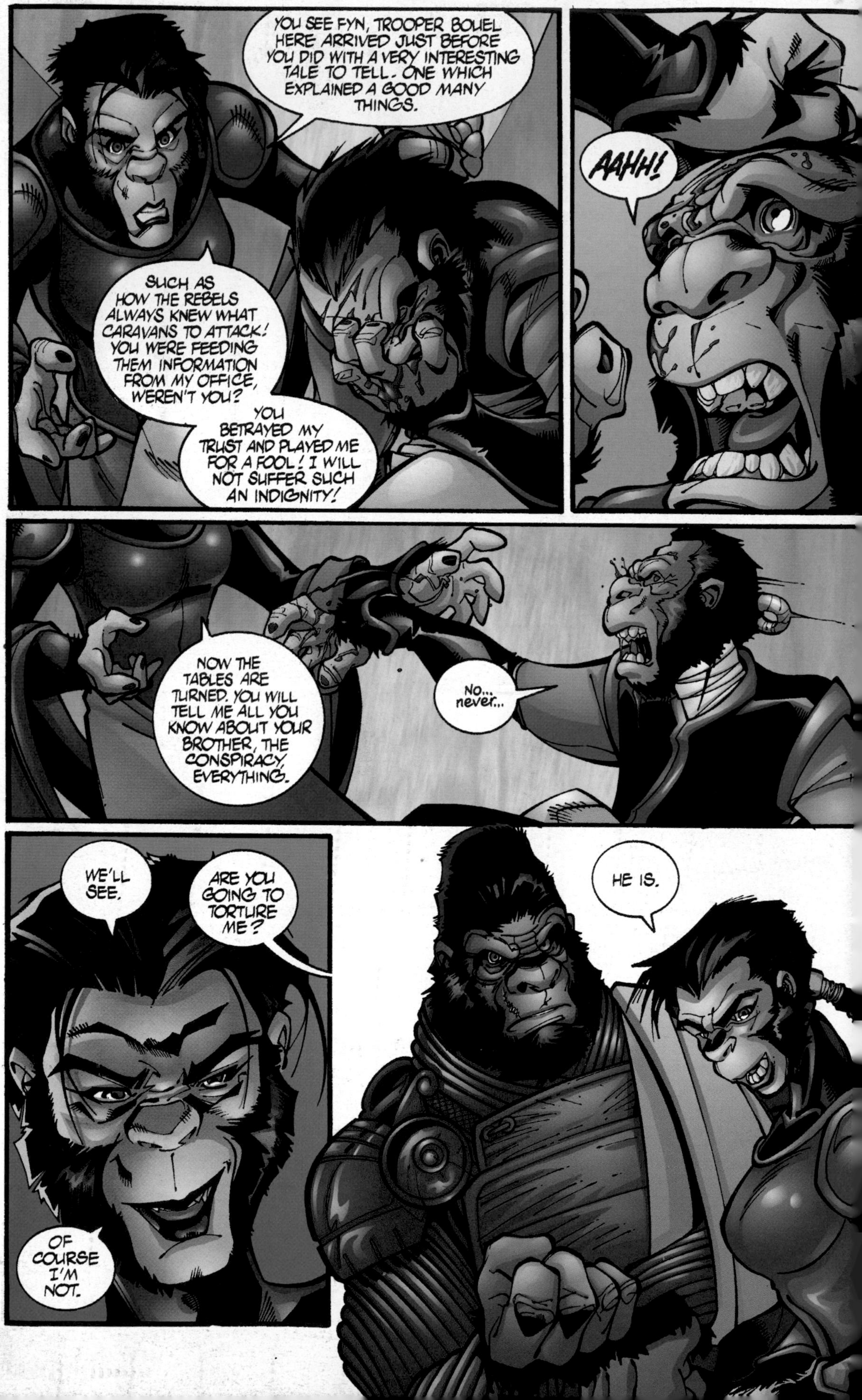
YOU SEE FYN, TROOPER BOUEL HERE ARRIVED JUST BEFORE YOU DID WITH A VERY INTERESTING TALE TO TELL. ONE WHICH EXPLAINED A GOOD MANY THINGS.
SUCH AS HOW THE REBELS ALWAYS KNEW WHAT CARAVANS TO ATTACK! YOU WERE FEEDING THEM INFORMATION FROM MY OFFICE, WEREN'T YOU?
YOU BETRAYED MY TRUST AND PLAYED ME FOR A FOOL! I WILL NOT SUFFER SUCH AN INDIGNITY!
AAHH!
NOW THE TABLES ARE TURNED. YOU WILL TELL ME ALL YOU KNOW ABOUT YOUR BROTHER, THE CONSPIRACY, EVERYTHING.
No... never...
ARE YOU GOING TO TORTURE ME?
WE'LL SEE.
OF COURSE I'M NOT.
HE IS.

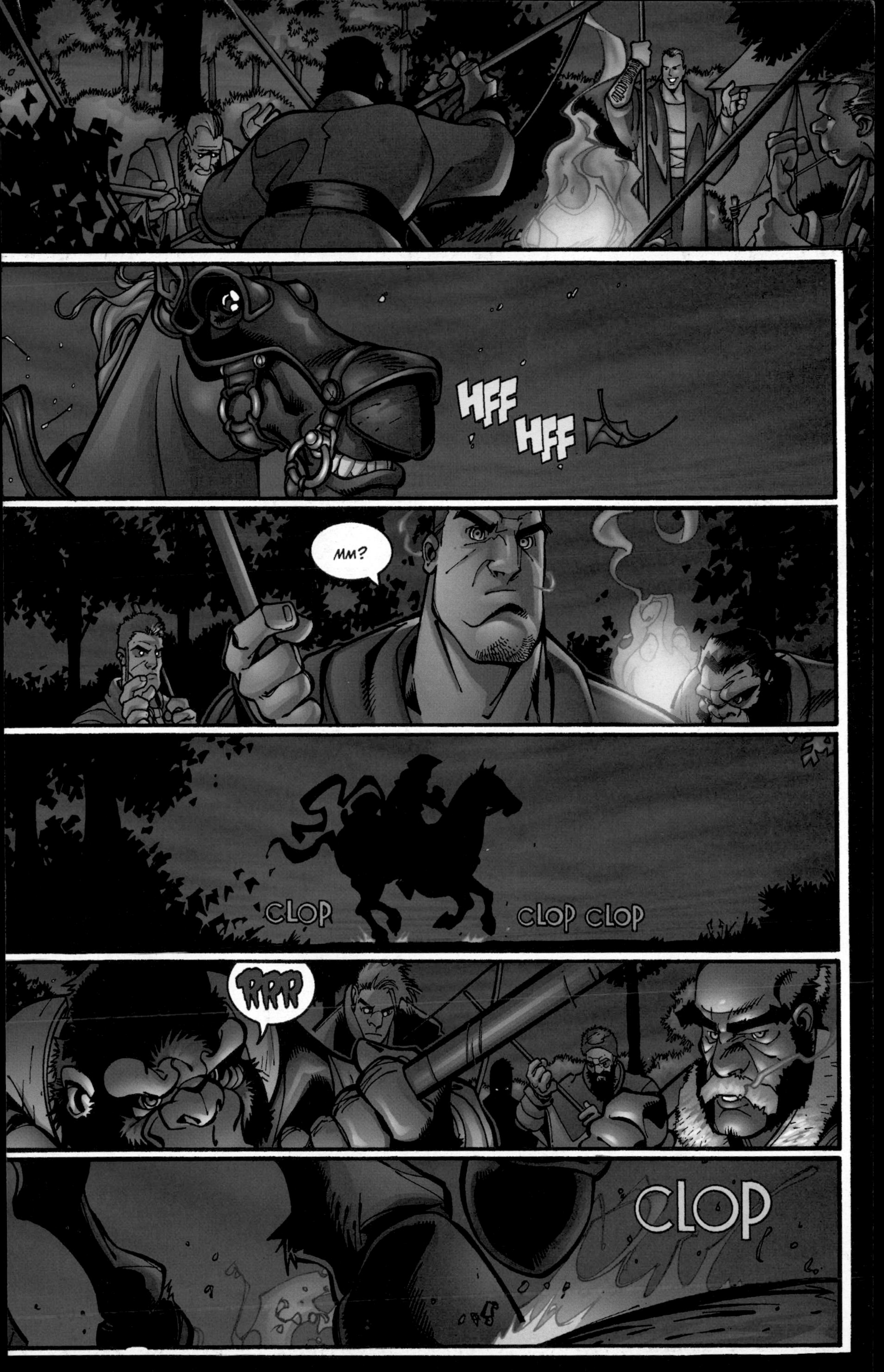
HFF HFF
MM?
CLOP
CLOP CLOP
RRRR
CLOP

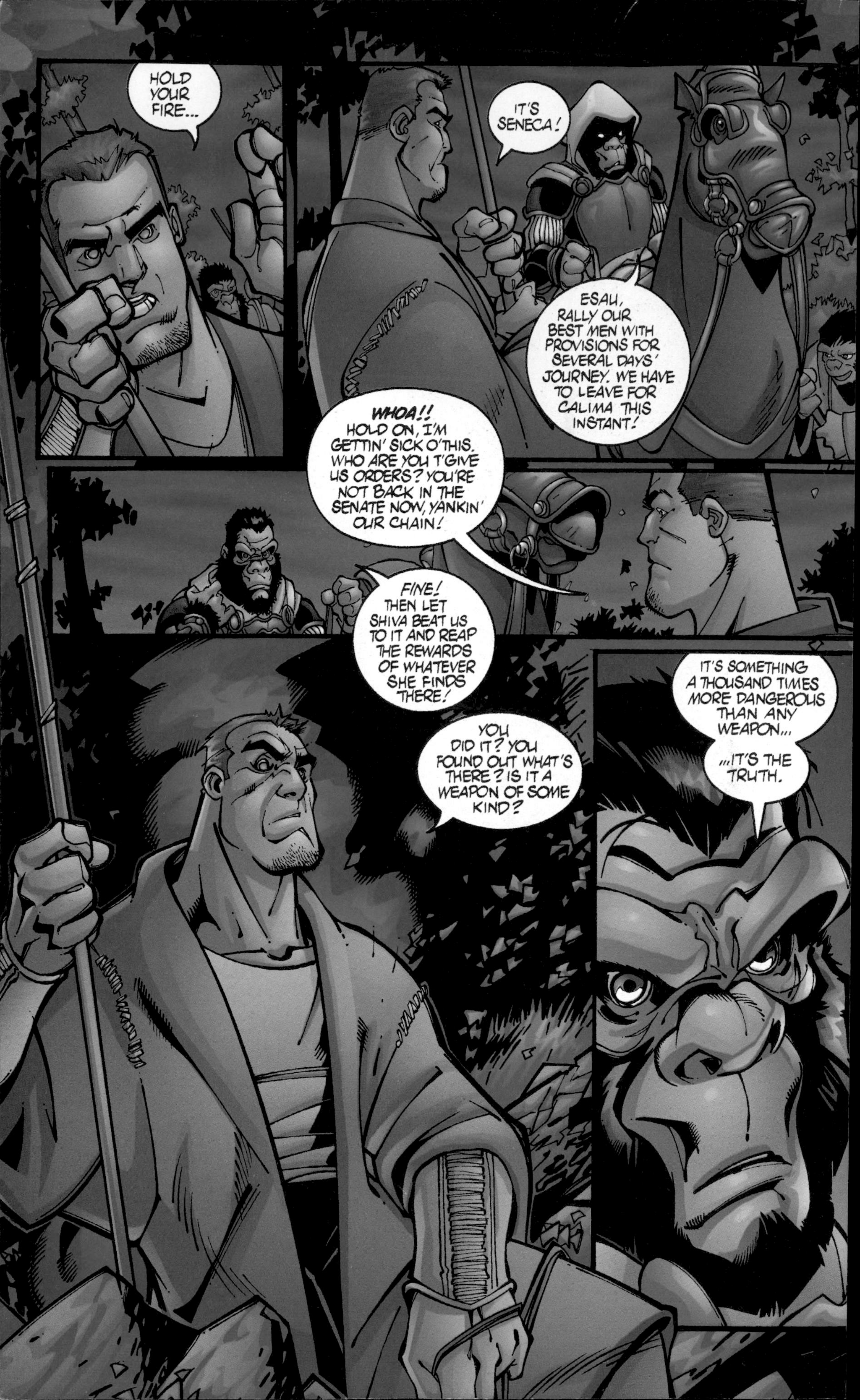

HOLD YOUR FIRE...
IT'S SENECA!
ESAU, RALLY OUR BEST MEN WITH PROVISIONS FOR SEVERAL DAYS' JOURNEY. WE HAVE TO LEAVE FOR CALIMA THIS INSTANT!
WHOA!! HOLD ON, I'M GETTIN' SICK O'THIS. WHO ARE YOU T'GIVE US ORDERS? YOU'RE NOT BACK IN THE SENATE NOW, YANKIN' OUR CHAIN!
FINE! THEN LET SHIVA BEAT US TO IT AND REAP THE REWARDS OF WHATEVER SHE FINDS THERE!
YOU DID IT? YOU FOUND OUT WHAT'S THERE? IS IT A WEAPON OF SOME KIND?
IT'S SOMETHING A THOUSAND TIMES MORE DANGEROUS THAN ANY WEAPON...
...IT'S THE TRUTH.

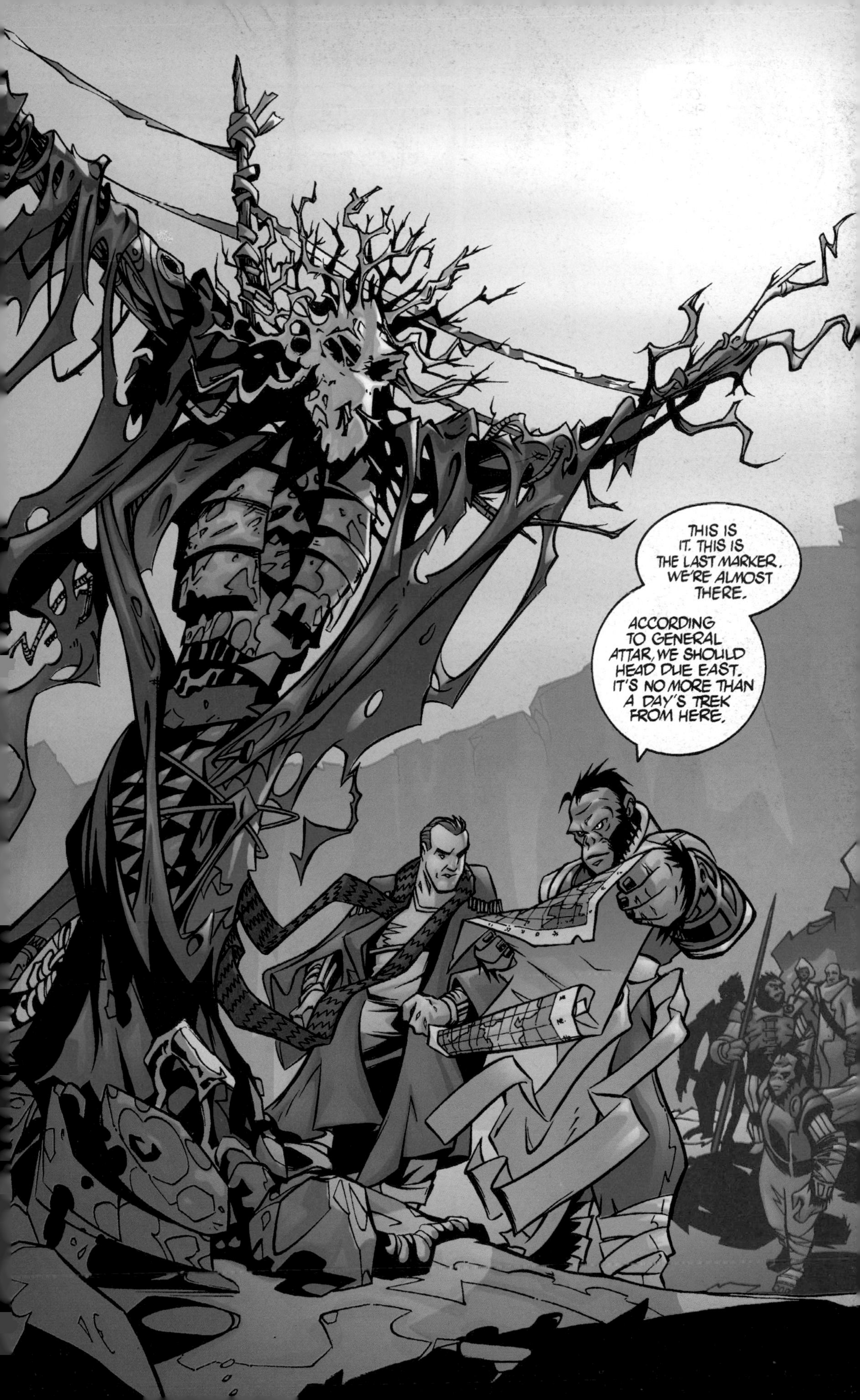
THIS IS IT. THIS IS THE LAST MARKER. WE'RE ALMOST THERE.
ACCORDING TO GENERAL ATTAR, WE SHOULD HEAD DUE EAST. IT'S NO MORE THAN A DAY'S TREK FROM HERE.

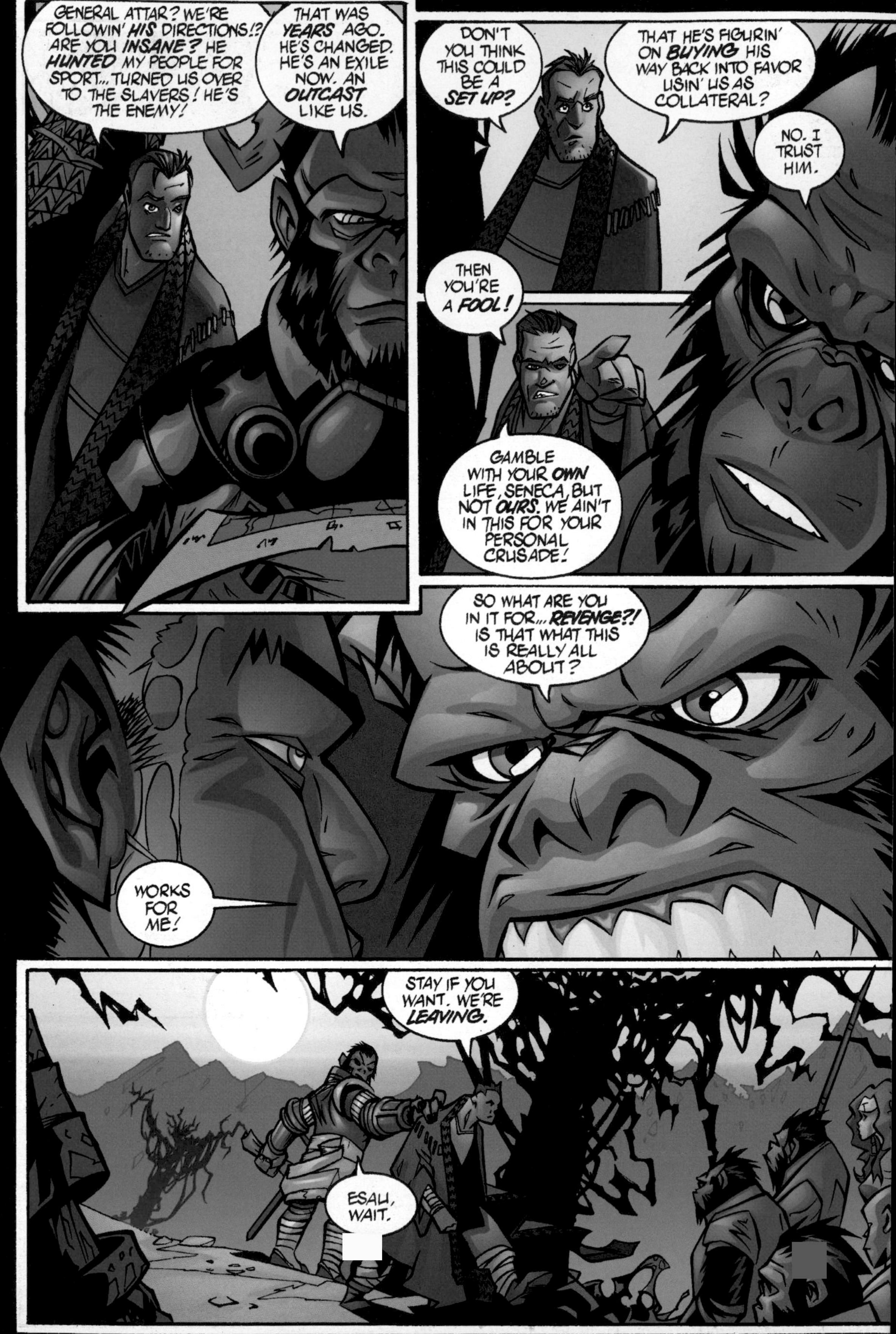
GENERAL ATTAR? WE'RE FOLLOWIN' HIS DIRECTIONS!? ARE YOU INSANE? HE HUNTED MY PEOPLE FOR SPORT... TURNED US OVER TO THE SLAVERS! HE'S THE ENEMY!
THAT WAS YEARS AGO. HE'S CHANGED. HE'S AN EXILE NOW. AN OUTCAST LIKE US.
DON'T YOU THINK THIS COULD BE A SET UP?
THAT HE'S FIGURIN' ON BUYING HIS WAY BACK INTO FAVOR USIN' US AS COLLATERAL?
NO. I TRUST HIM.
THEN YOU'RE A FOOL!
GAMBLE WITH YOUR OWN LIFE, SENECA, BUT NOT OURS. WE AIN'T IN THIS FOR YOUR PERSONAL CRUSADE!
SO WHAT ARE YOU IN IT FOR... REVENGE?! IS THAT WHAT THIS IS REALLY ALL ABOUT?
WORKS FOR ME!
STAY IF YOU WANT. WE'RE LEAVING.
ESAU, WAIT.

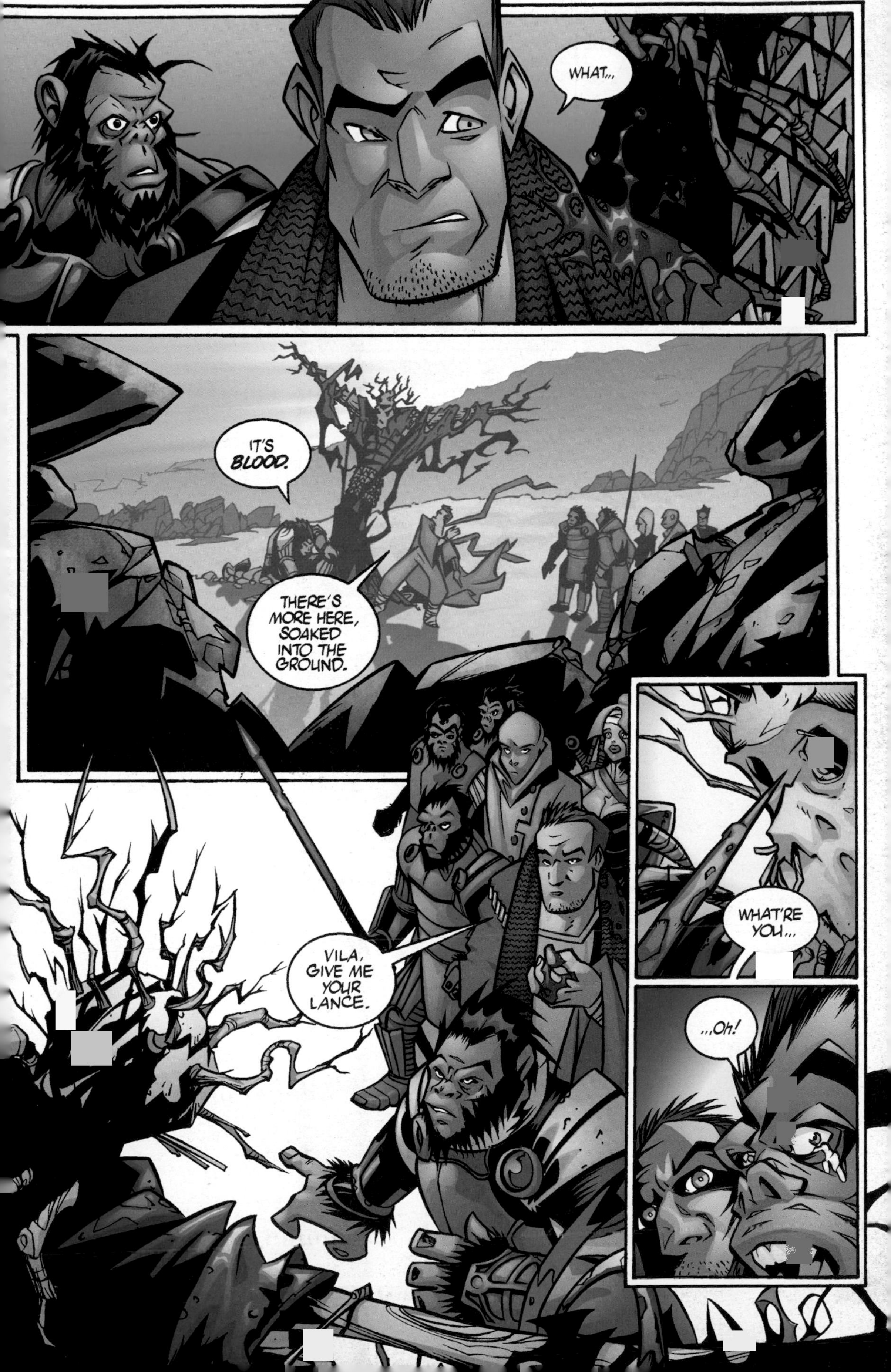
WHAT...
IT'S BLOOD.
THERE'S MORE HERE, SOAKED INTO THE GROUND.
VILA, GIVE ME YOUR LANCE.
WHAT'RE YOU...
...Oh!

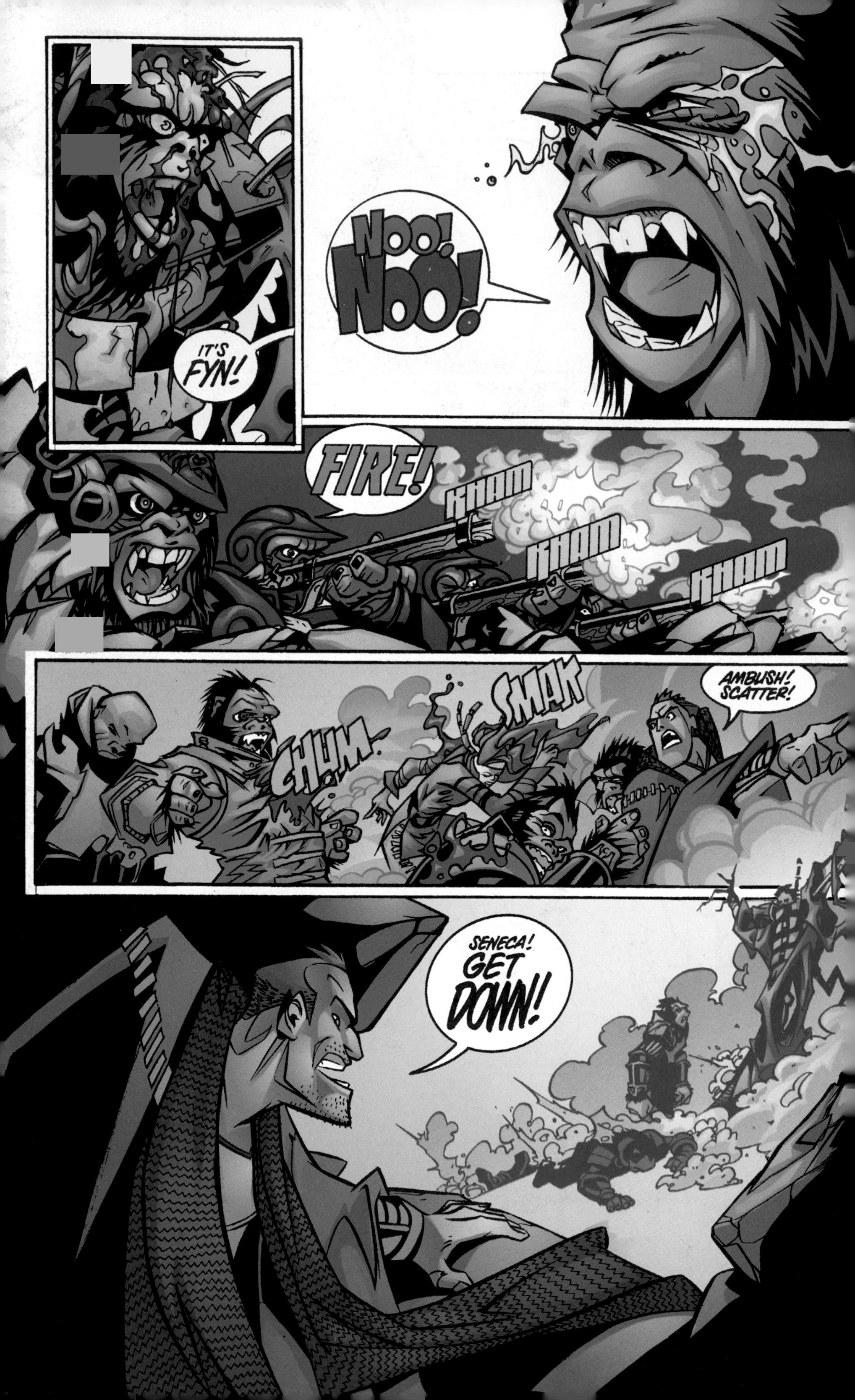
IT'S FYN!
NOO! NOO!
FIRE!
KHAM
KHAM
KHAM
CHUM
SMAK
AMBUSH! SCATTER!
SENECA! GET DOWN!

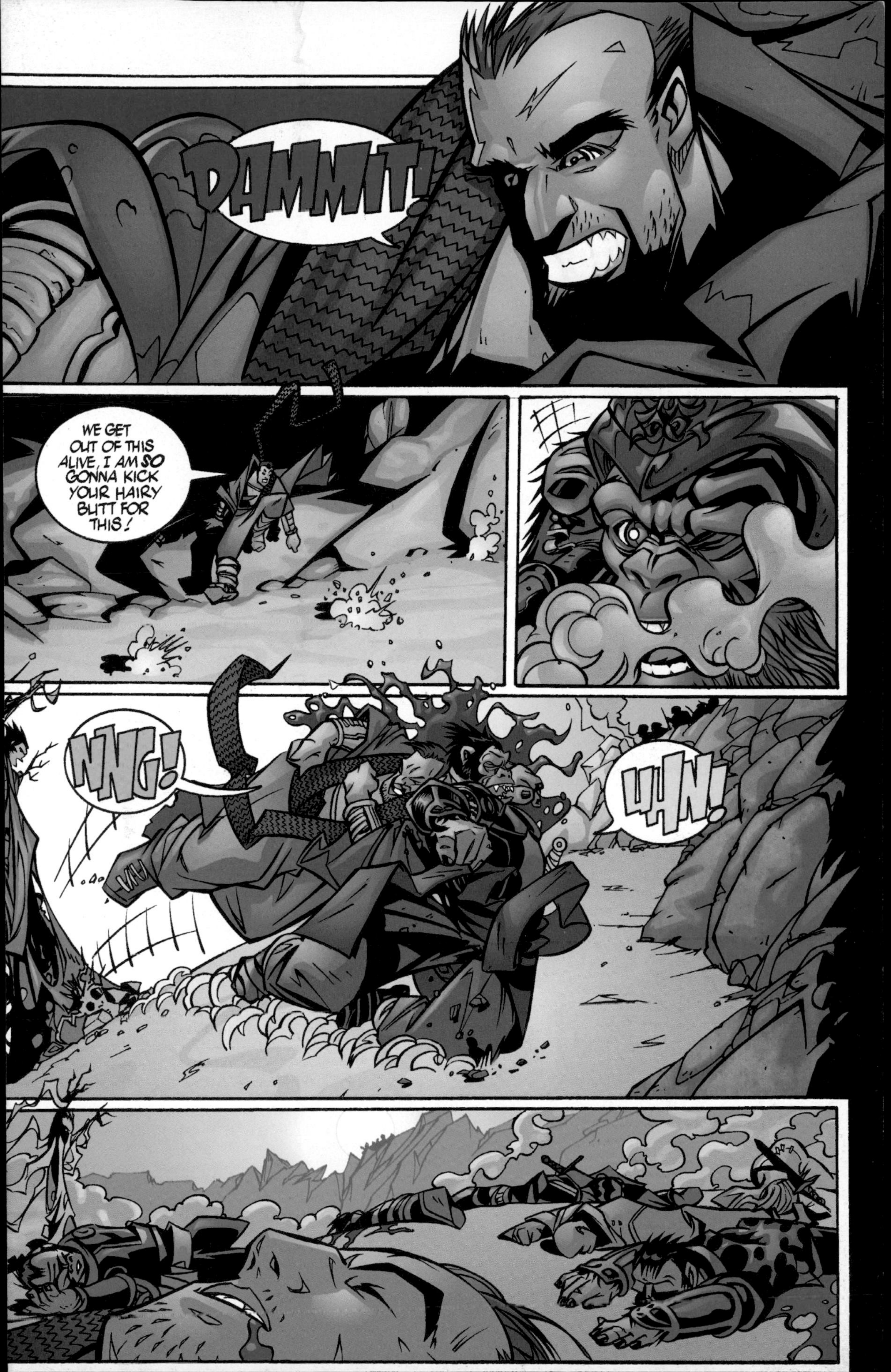
DAMMIT!
WE GET OUT OF THIS ALIVE, I AM SO GONNA KICK YOUR HAIRY BUTT FOR THIS!
NNG!
UHN!

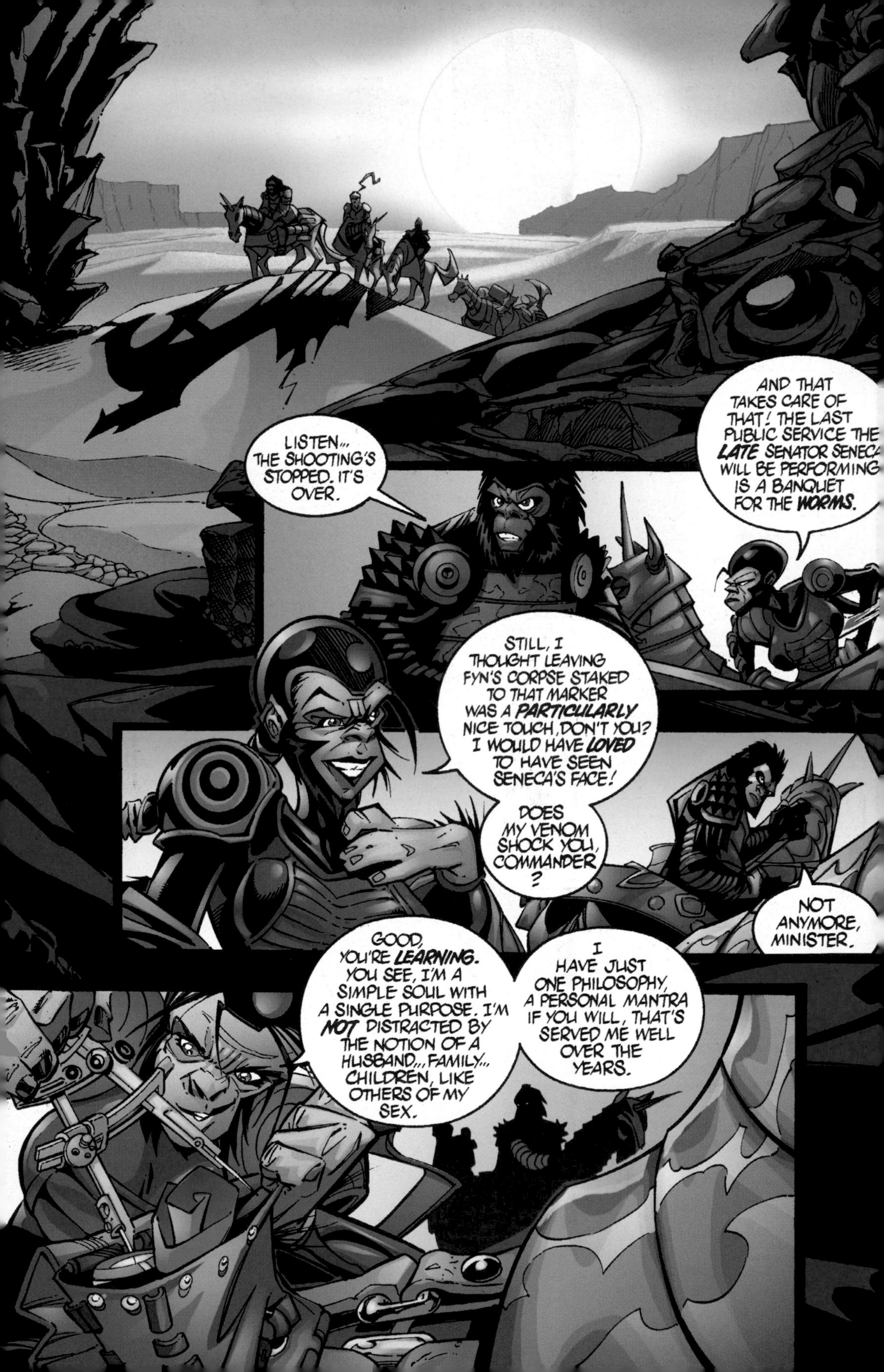
LISTEN... THE SHOOTING'S STOPPED. IT'S OVER.
AND THAT TAKES CARE OF THAT! THE LAST PUBLIC SERVICE THE LATE SENATOR SENECA WILL BE PERFORMING IS A BANQUET FOR THE WORMS.
STILL, I THOUGHT LEAVING FYN'S CORPSE STAKED TO THAT MARKER WAS A PARTICULARLY NICE TOUCH, DON'T YOU? I WOULD HAVE LOVED TO HAVE SEEN SENECA'S FACE!
DOES MY VENOM SHOCK YOU, COMMANDER?
NOT ANYMORE, MINISTER.
GOOD, YOU'RE LEARNING. YOU SEE, I'M A SIMPLE SOUL WITH A SINGLE PURPOSE. I'M NOT DISTRACTED BY THE NOTION OF A HUSBAND... FAMILY... CHILDREN, LIKE OTHERS OF MY SEX.
I HAVE JUST ONE PHILOSOPHY, A PERSONAL MANTRA IF YOU WILL, THAT'S SERVED ME WELL OVER THE YEARS.

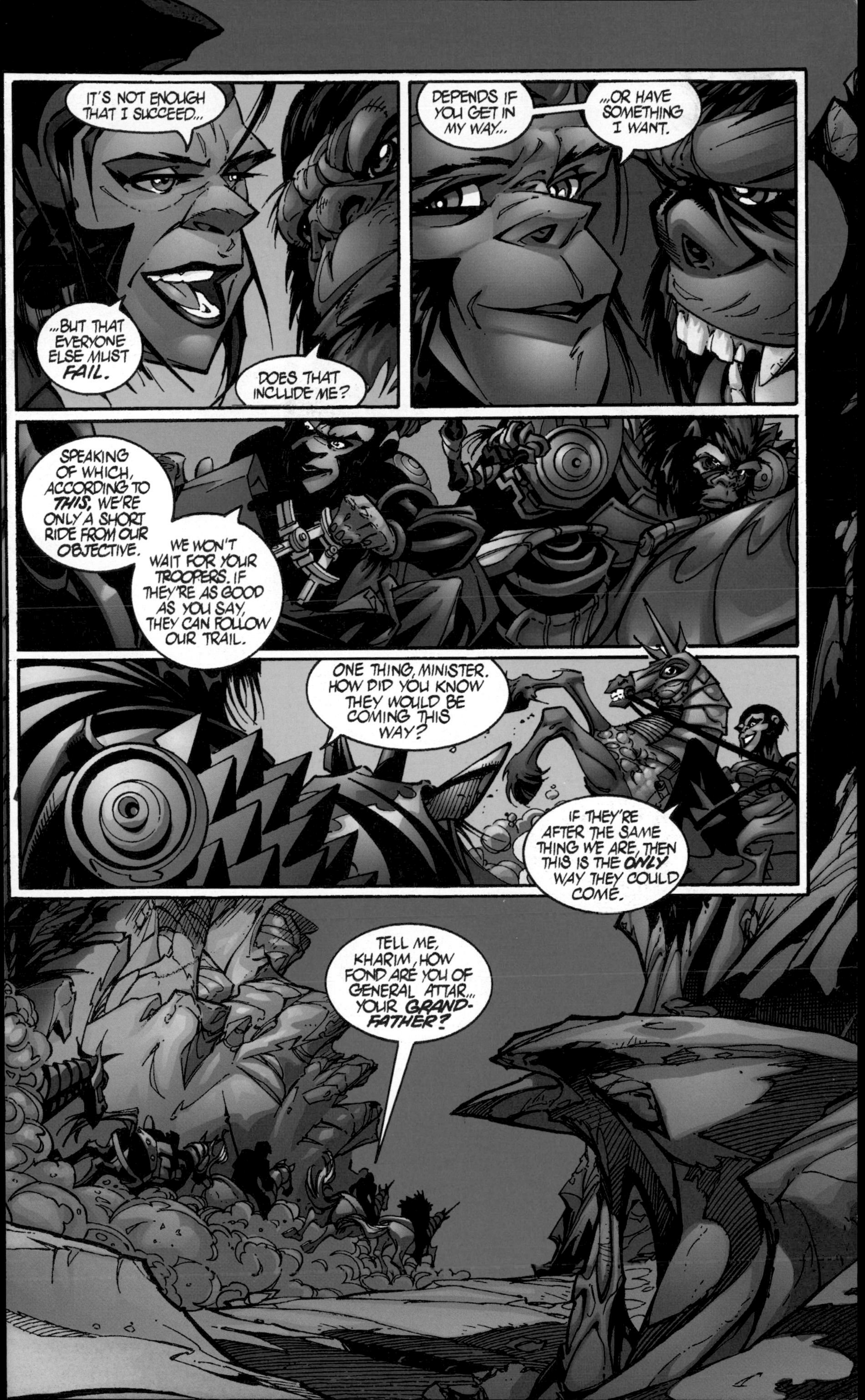
IT'S NOT ENOUGH THAT I SUCCEED...
...BUT THAT EVERYONE ELSE MUST FAIL.
DOES THAT INCLUDE ME?
DEPENDS IF YOU GET IN MY WAY...
...OR HAVE SOMETHING I WANT.
SPEAKING OF WHICH, ACCORDING TO THIS, WE'RE ONLY A SHORT RIDE FROM OUR OBJECTIVE.
WE WON'T WAIT FOR YOUR TROOPERS. IF THEY'RE AS GOOD AS YOU SAY, THEY CAN FOLLOW OUR TRAIL.
ONE THING, MINISTER. HOW DID YOU KNOW THEY WOULD BE COMING THIS WAY?
IF THEY'RE AFTER THE SAME THING WE ARE, THEN THIS IS THE ONLY WAY THEY COULD COME.
TELL ME, KHARIM, HOW FOND ARE YOU OF GENERAL ATTAR... YOUR GRAND-FATHER?

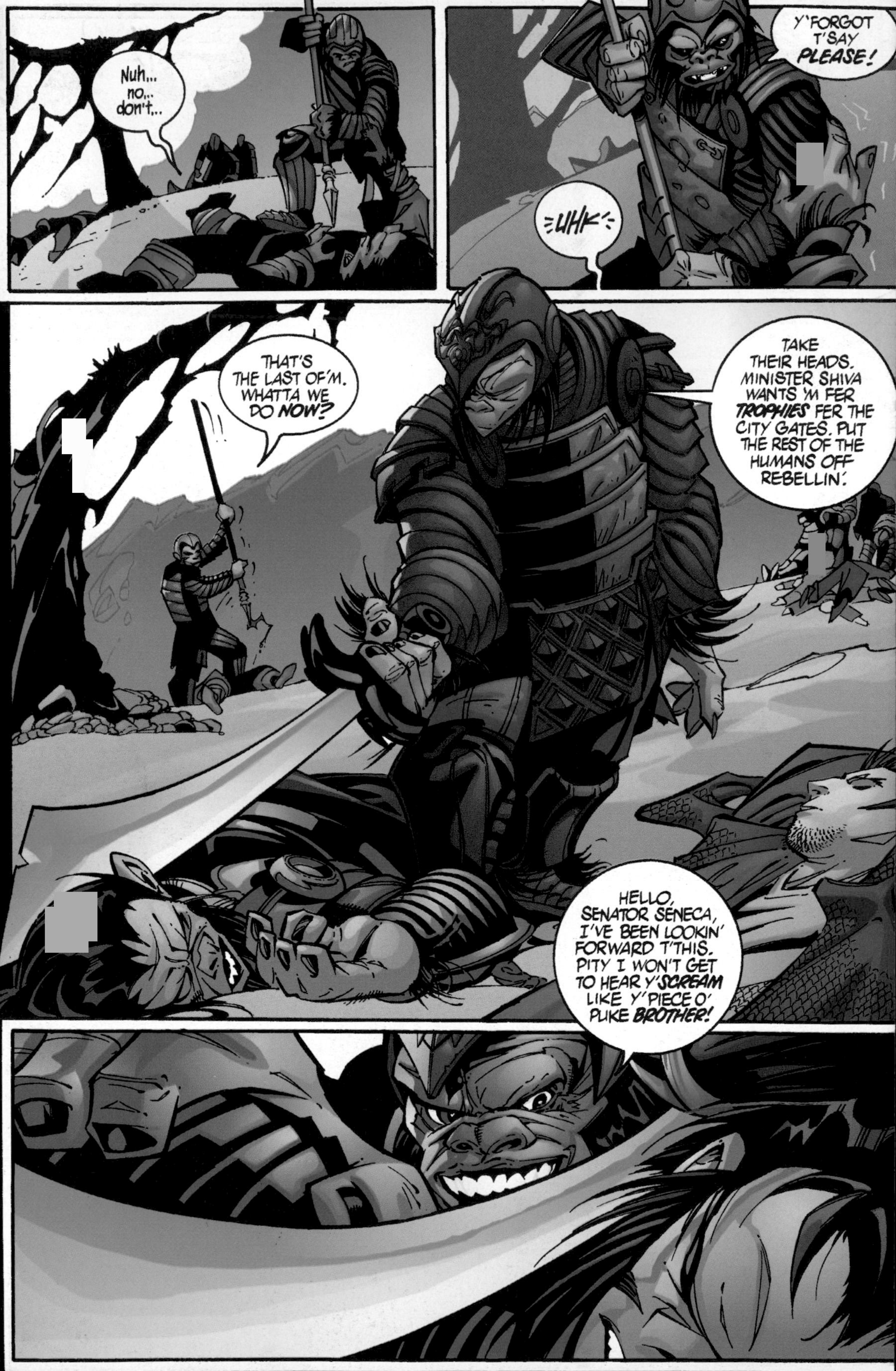
Nuh... no... don't...
Y'FORGOT T'SAY PLEASE!
UHK
THAT'S THE LAST OF'M. WHATTA WE DO NOW?
TAKE THEIR HEADS. MINISTER SHIVA WANTS 'M FER TROPHIES FER THE CITY GATES. PUT THE REST OF THE HUMANS OFF REBELLIN'.
HELLO, SENATOR SENECA, I'VE BEEN LOOKIN' FORWARD T'THIS. PITY I WON'T GET TO HEAR Y'SCREAM LIKE Y'PIECE O' PUKE BROTHER!

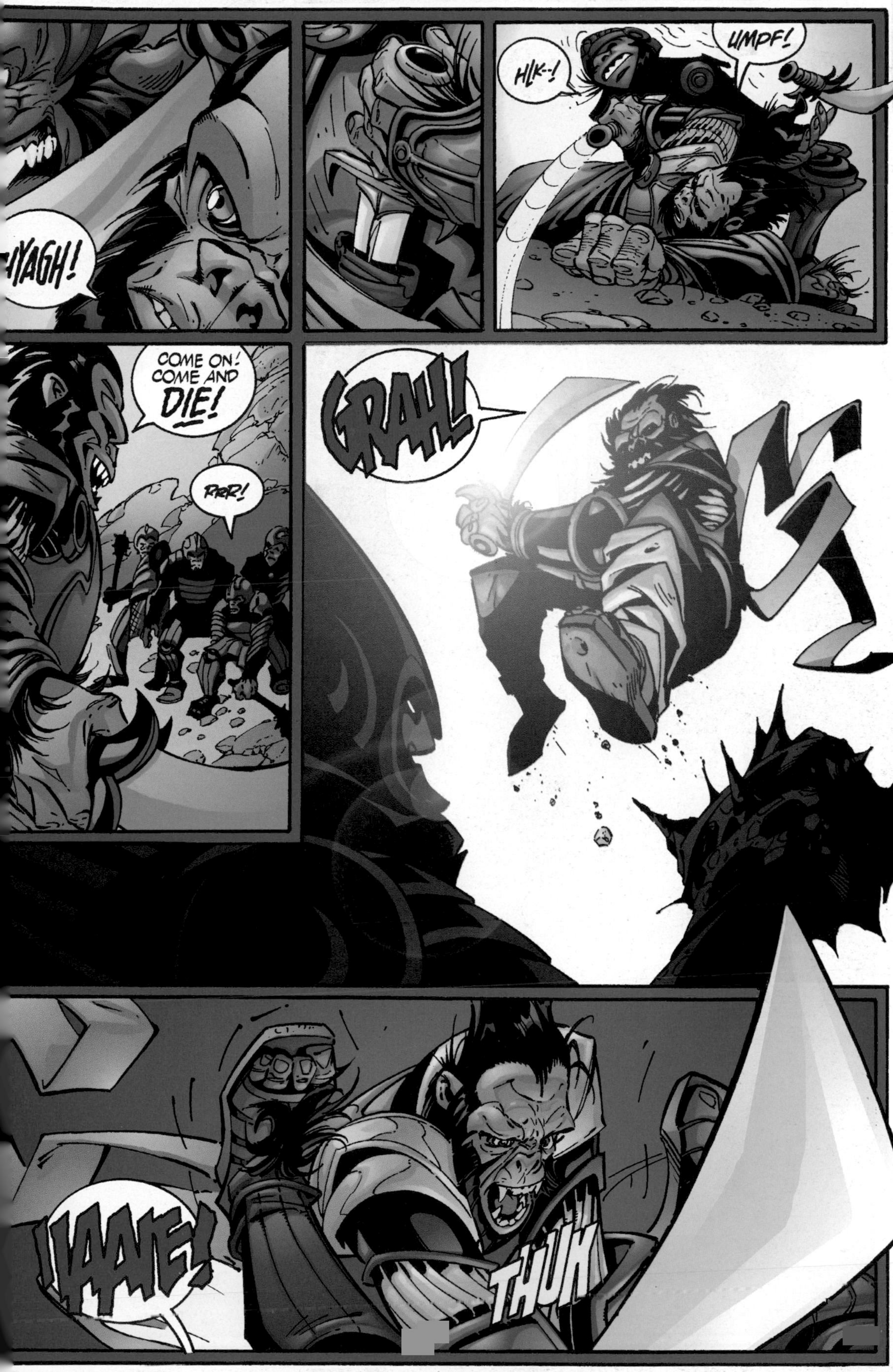

HIYAGH!
HLK-!
UMPF!
COME ON! COME AND DIE!
RRR!
GRAH!
YAAIE!
THUK

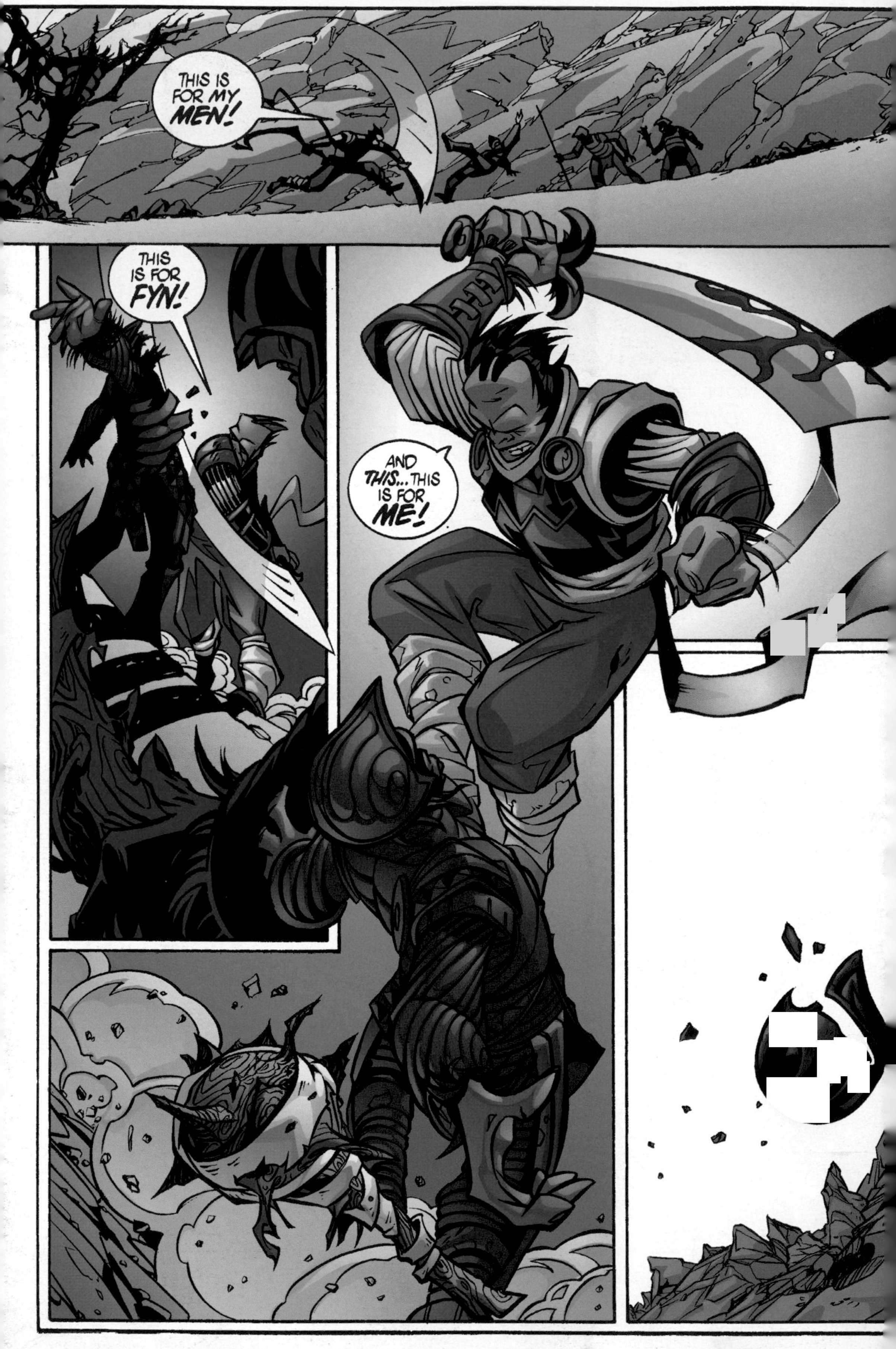
THIS IS FOR MY MEN!
THIS IS FOR FYN!
AND THIS... THIS IS FOR ME!

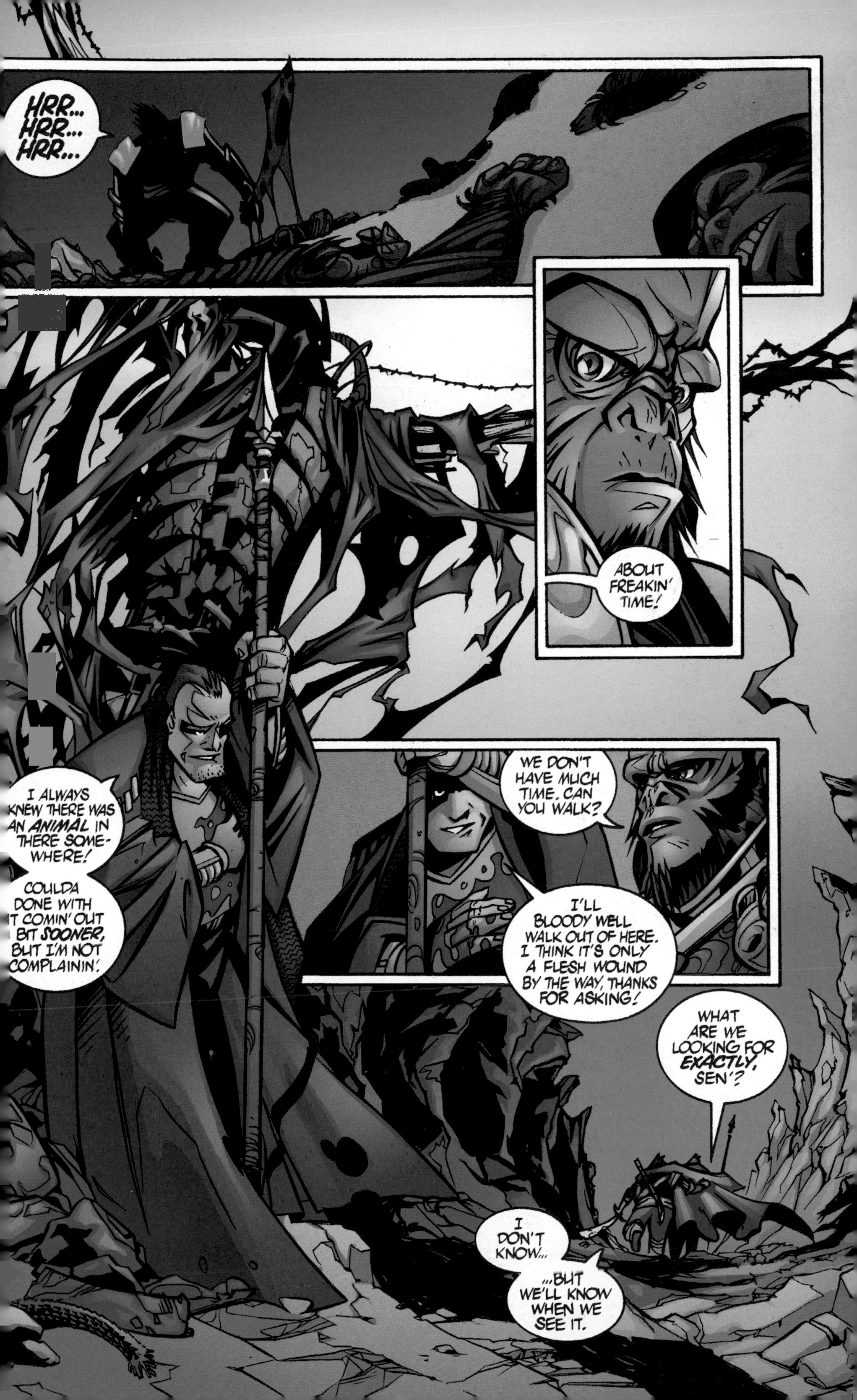
HRR... HRR... HRR...
ABOUT FREAKIN' TIME!
I ALWAYS KNEW THERE WAS AN ANIMAL IN THERE SOME- WHERE!
COULDA DONE WITH T COMIN' OUT BIT SOONER, BUT I'M NOT COMPLAININ'.
WE DON'T HAVE MUCH TIME. CAN YOU WALK?
I'LL BLOODY WELL WALK OUT OF HERE. I THINK IT'S ONLY A FLESH WOUND BY THE WAY, THANKS FOR ASKING!
WHAT ARE WE LOOKING FOR EXACTLY, SEN'?
I DON'T KNOW...
...BUT WE'LL KNOW WHEN WE SEE IT.

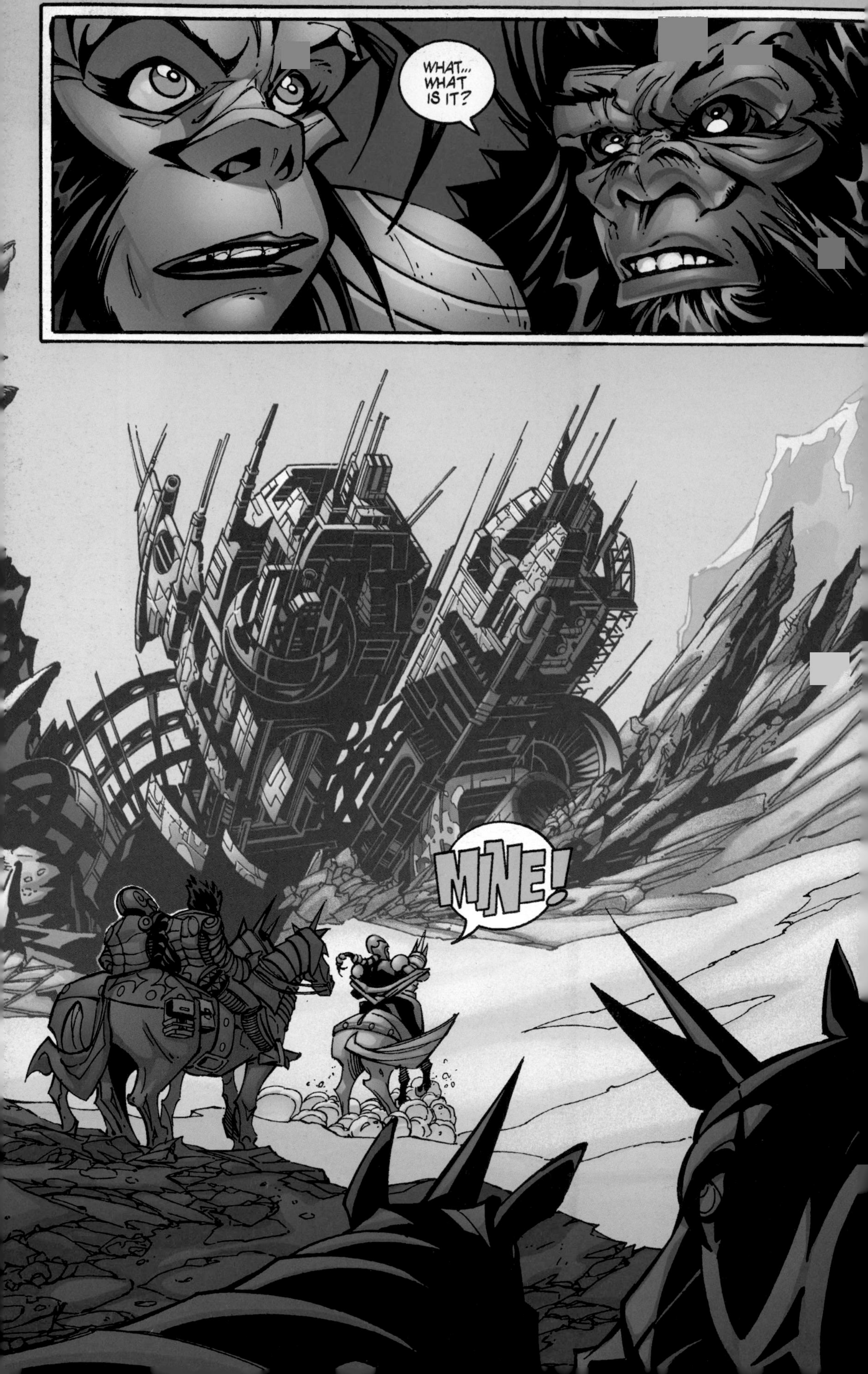
WHAT... WHAT IS IT?
MINE!

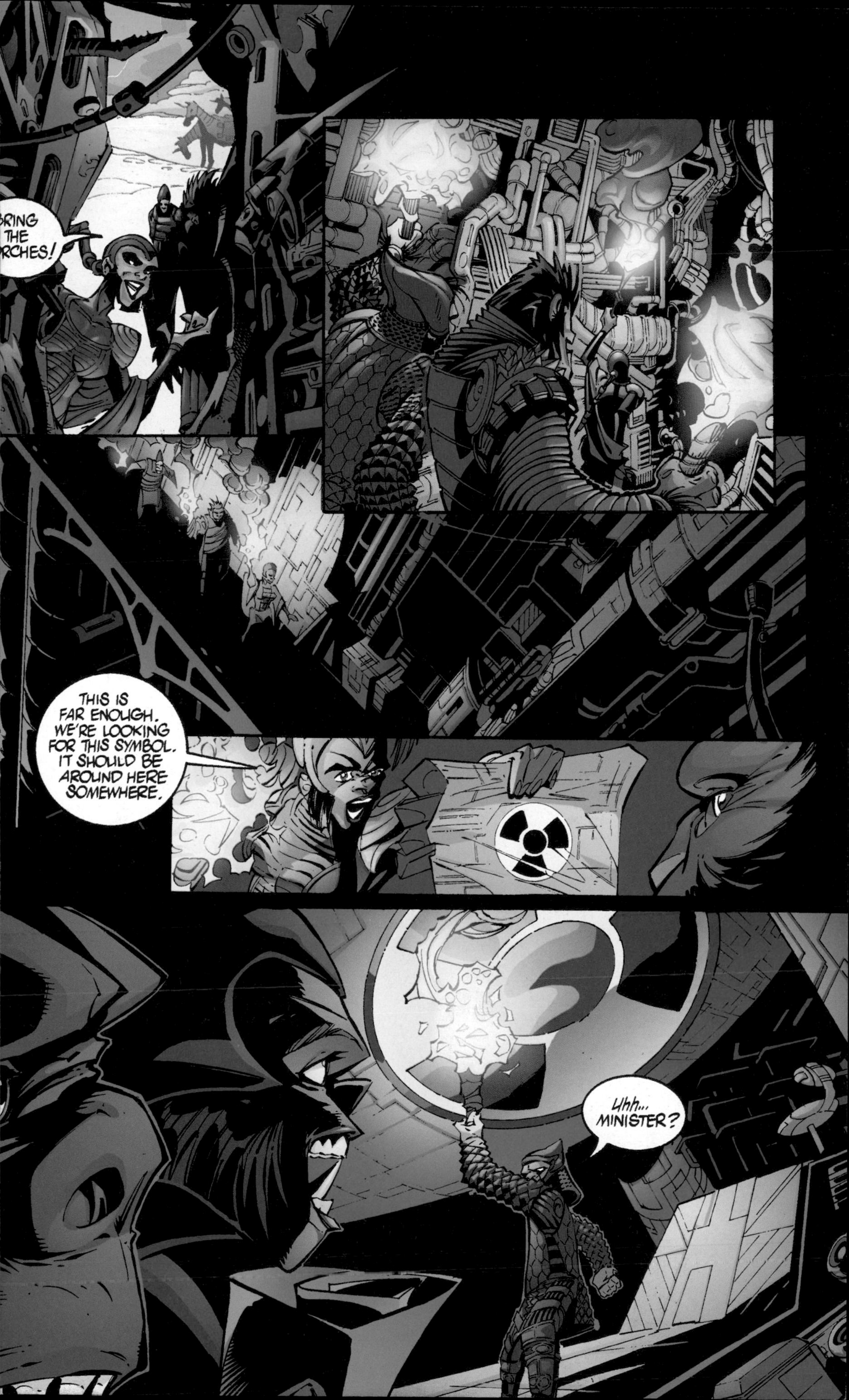
BRING THE TORCHES!
THIS IS FAR ENOUGH. WE'RE LOOKING FOR THIS SYMBOL. IT SHOULD BE AROUND HERE SOMEWHERE.
Uhh... MINISTER?

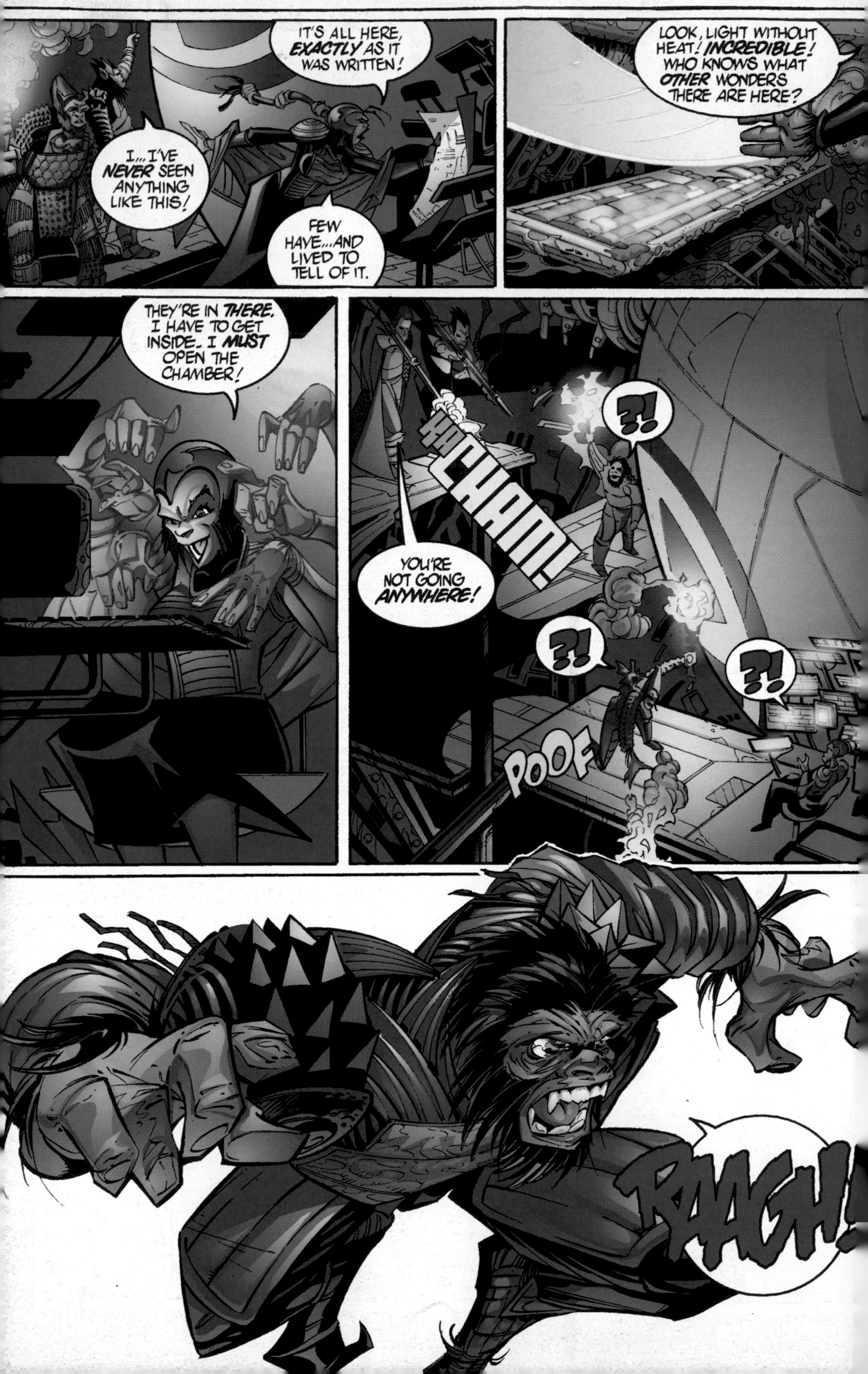
IT'S ALL HERE, EXACTLY AS IT WAS WRITTEN!
I... I'VE NEVER SEEN ANYTHING LIKE THIS!
FEW HAVE... AND LIVED TO TELL OF IT.
LOOK, LIGHT WITHOUT HEAT! INCREDIBLE! WHO KNOWS WHAT OTHER WONDERS THERE ARE HERE?
THEY'RE IN THERE. I HAVE TO GET INSIDE. I MUST OPEN THE CHAMBER!
KKCHAM!
?!
YOU'RE NOT GOING ANYWHERE!
?!
?!
POOF
RAAGH!

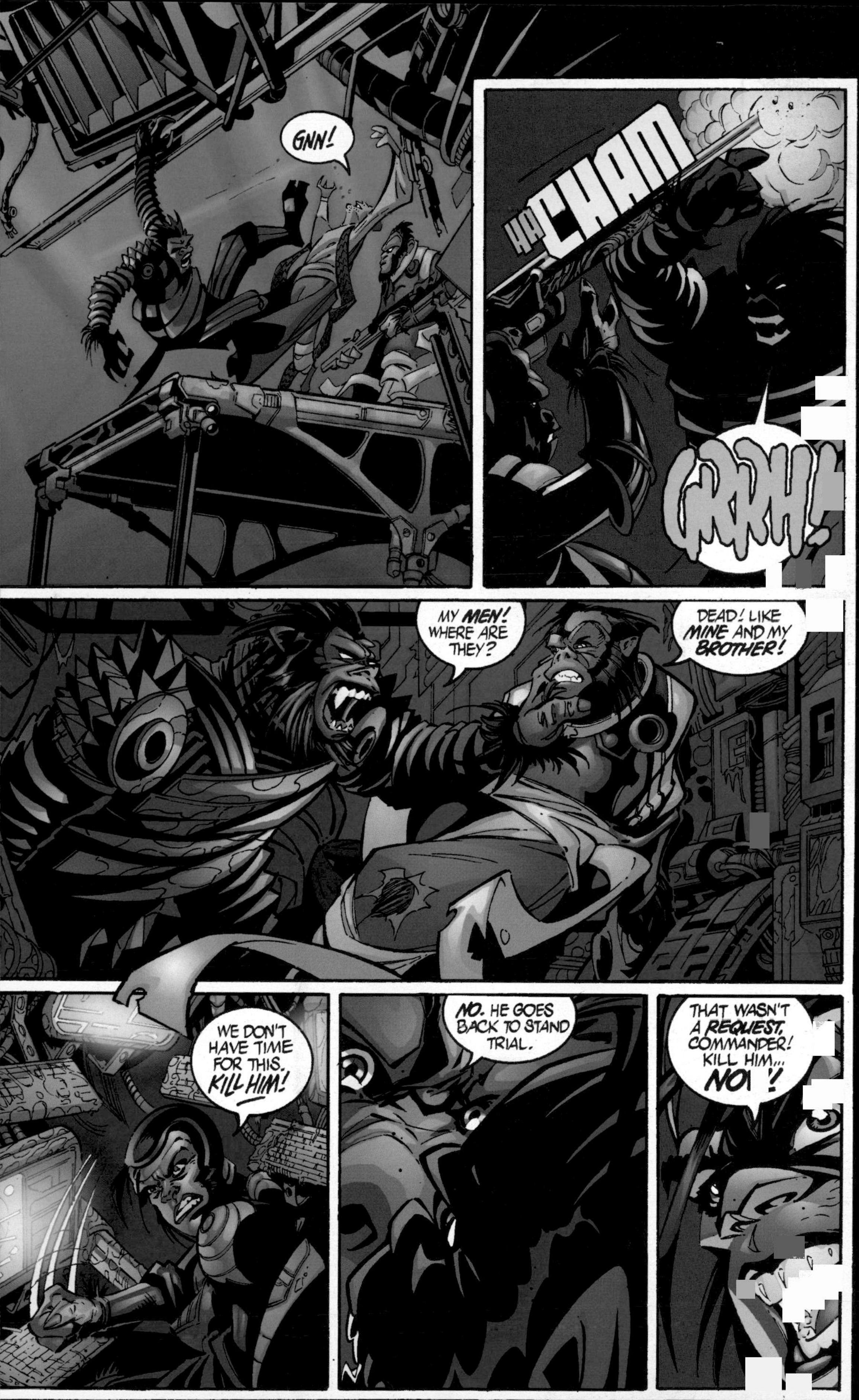
GNN!
KACHAM
GRRH!
MY MEN! WHERE ARE THEY?
DEAD! LIKE MINE AND MY BROTHER!
WE DON'T HAVE TIME FOR THIS. KILL HIM!
NO. HE GOES BACK TO STAND TRIAL.
THAT WASN'T A REQUEST, COMMANDER! KILL HIM...

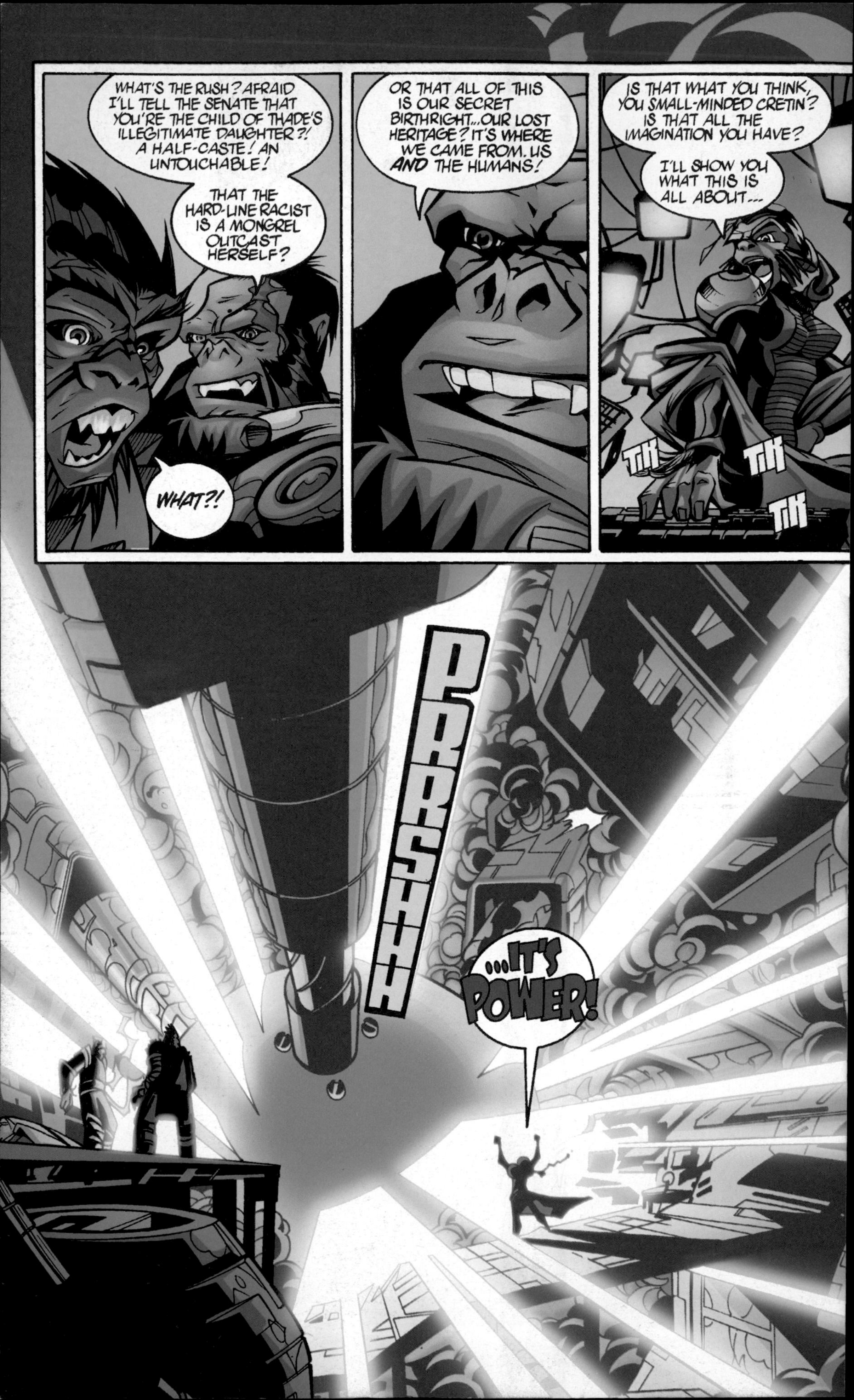
WHAT'S THE RUSH? AFRAID I'LL TELL THE SENATE THAT YOU'RE THE CHILD OF THADE'S ILLEGITIMATE DAUGHTER?! A HALF-CASTE! AN UNTOUCHABLE!
THAT THE HARD-LINE RACIST IS A MONGREL OUTCAST HERSELF?
WHAT?!
OR THAT ALL OF THIS IS OUR SECRET BIRTHRIGHT...OUR LOST HERITAGE? IT'S WHERE WE CAME FROM. US AND THE HUMANS!
IS THAT WHAT YOU THINK, YOU SMALL-MINDED CRETIN? IS THAT ALL THE IMAGINATION YOU HAVE?
I'LL SHOW YOU WHAT THIS IS ALL ABOUT...
TIK
TIK
TIK
PRRSHHH
...IT'S POWER!

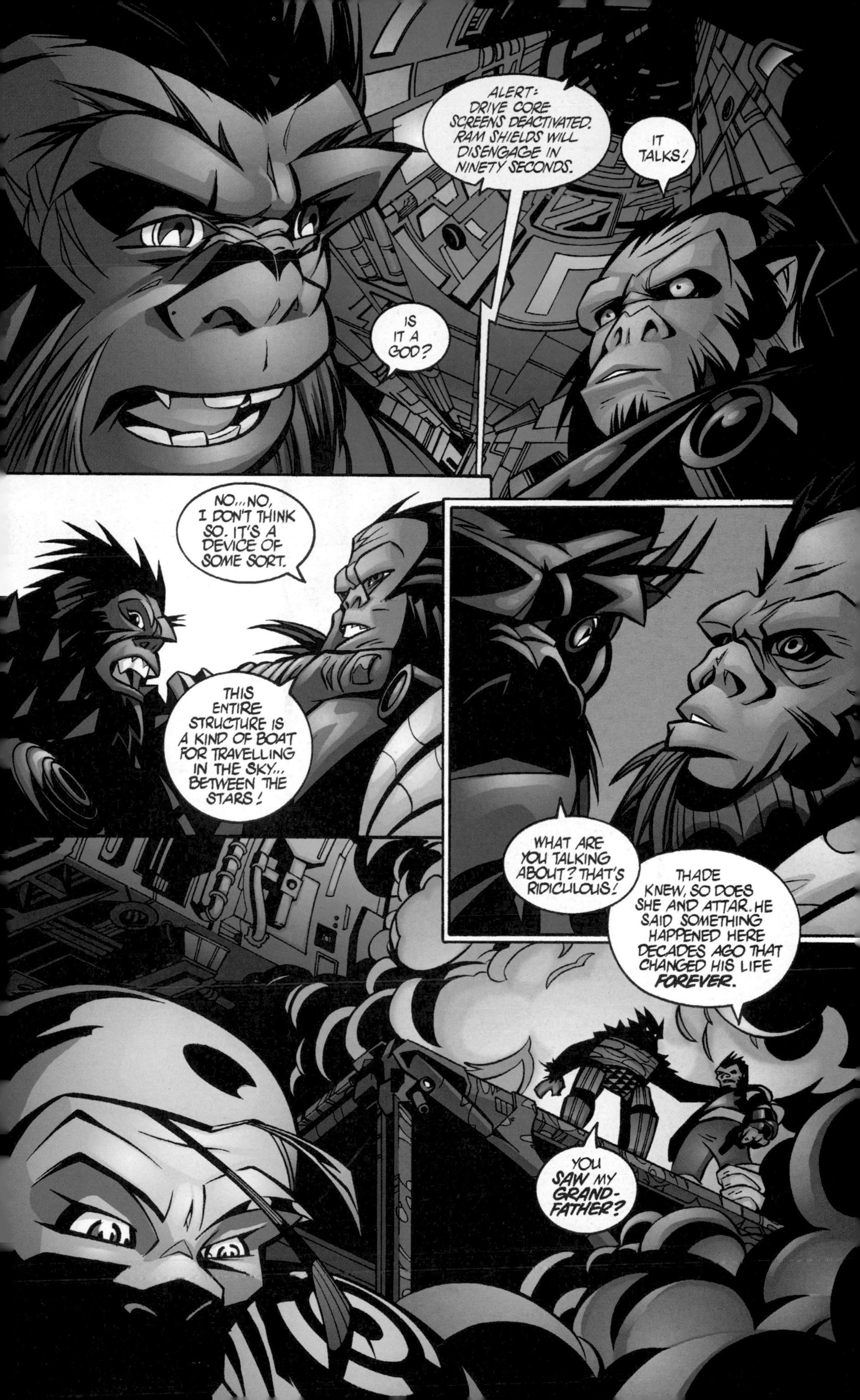
ALERT: DRIVE CORE SCREENS DEACTIVATED. RAM SHIELDS WILL DISENGAGE IN NINETY SECONDS.
IT TALKS!
IS IT A GOD?
NO... NO, I DON'T THINK SO. IT'S A DEVICE OF SOME SORT.
THIS ENTIRE STRUCTURE IS A KIND OF BOAT FOR TRAVELLING IN THE SKY... BETWEEN THE STARS!
WHAT ARE YOU TALKING ABOUT? THAT'S RIDICULOUS!
THADE KNEW, SO DOES SHE AND ATTAR. HE SAID SOMETHING HAPPENED HERE DECADES AGO THAT CHANGED HIS LIFE FOREVER.
YOU SAW MY GRAND-FATHER?

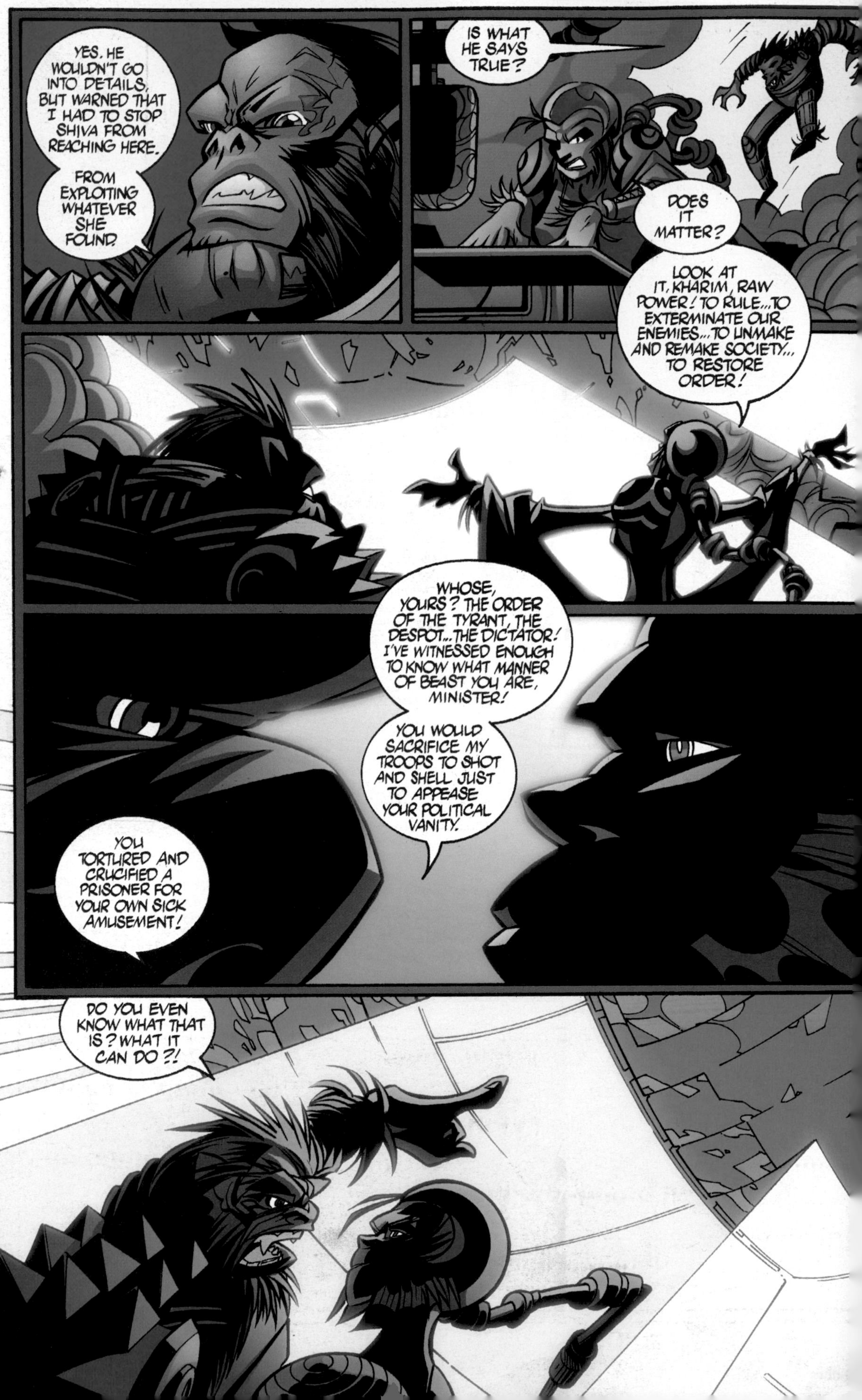
YES. HE WOULDN'T GO INTO DETAILS, BUT WARNED THAT I HAD TO STOP SHIVA FROM REACHING HERE.
FROM EXPLOITING WHATEVER SHE FOUND.
IS WHAT HE SAYS TRUE?
DOES IT MATTER?
LOOK AT IT, KHARIM, RAW POWER! TO RULE...TO EXTERMINATE OUR ENEMIES...TO UNMAKE AND REMAKE SOCIETY... TO RESTORE ORDER!
WHOSE, YOURS? THE ORDER OF THE TYRANT, THE DESPOT...THE DICTATOR! I'VE WITNESSED ENOUGH TO KNOW WHAT MANNER OF BEAST YOU ARE, MINISTER!
YOU WOULD SACRIFICE MY TROOPS TO SHOT AND SHELL JUST TO APPEASE YOUR POLITICAL VANITY.
YOU TORTURED AND CRUCIFIED A PRISONER FOR YOUR OWN SICK AMUSEMENT!
DO YOU EVEN KNOW WHAT THAT IS? WHAT IT CAN DO?!

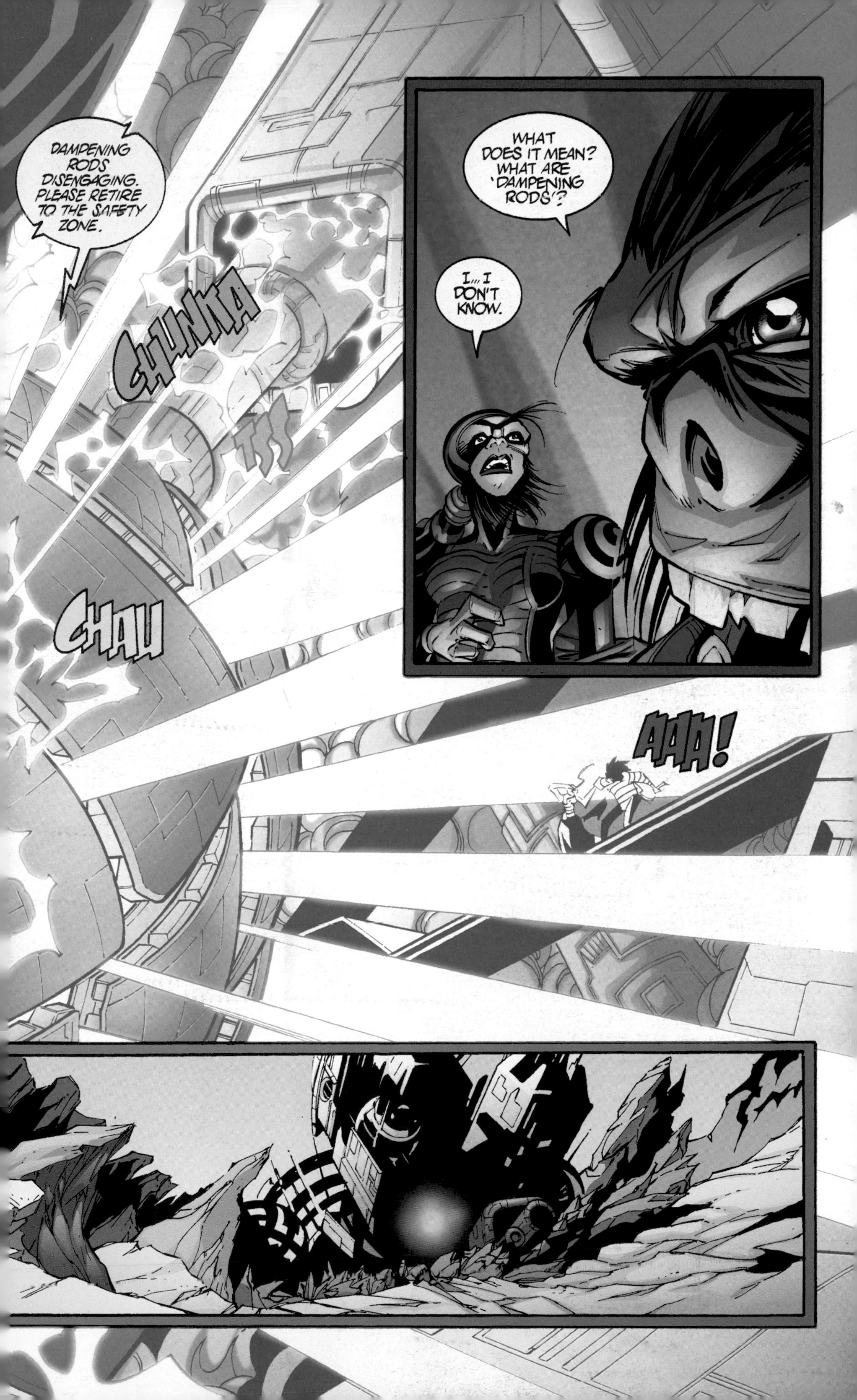
DAMPENING RODS DISENGAGING. PLEASE RETIRE TO THE SAFETY ZONE.
CHUNKA
TSS
CHAU
WHAT DOES IT MEAN? WHAT ARE 'DAMPENING RODS'?
I... I DON'T KNOW.
AAA!

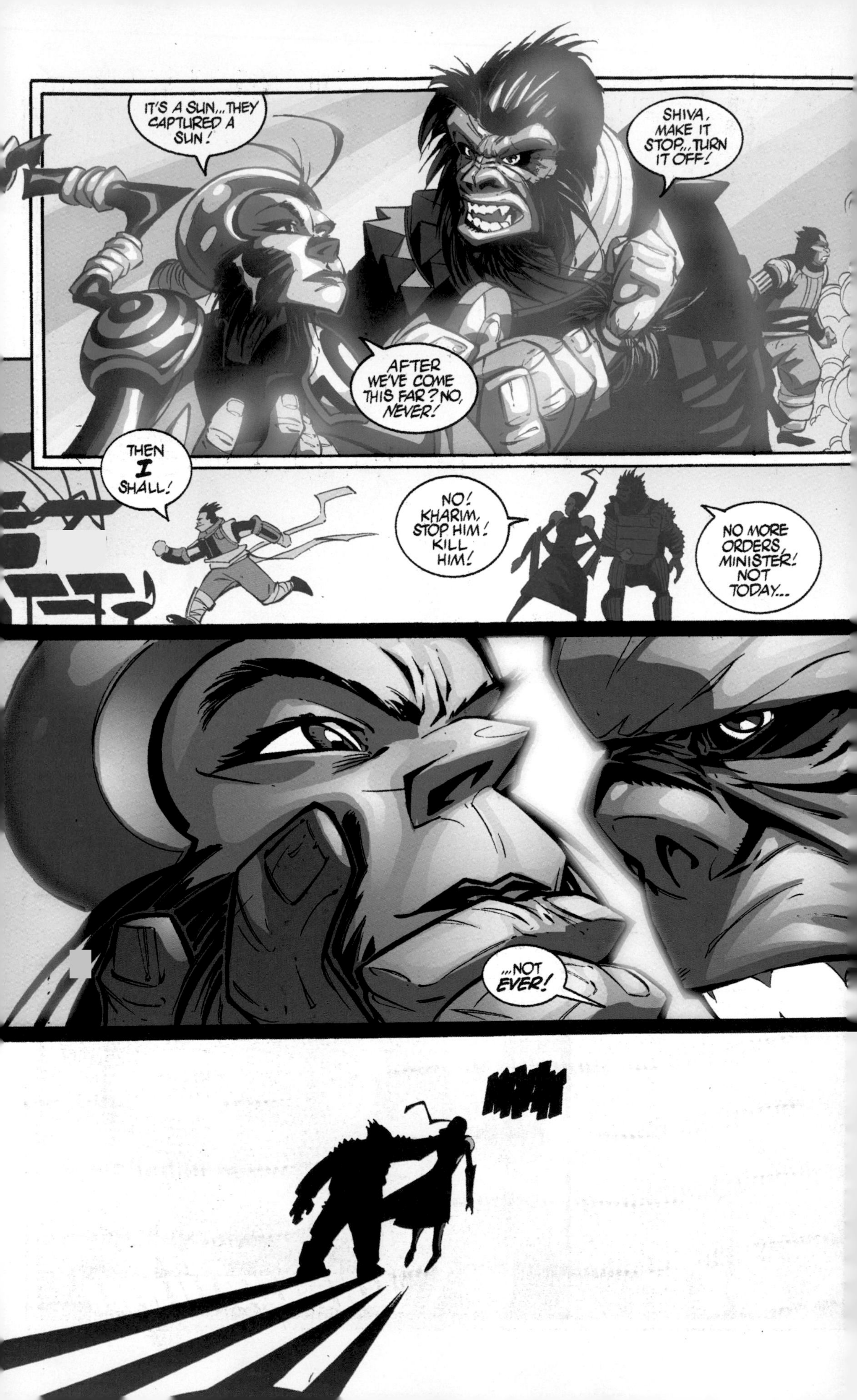
IT'S A SUN... THEY CAPTURED A SUN!
SHIVA, MAKE IT STOP... TURN IT OFF!
AFTER WE'VE COME THIS FAR? NO, NEVER!
THEN I SHALL!
NO! KHARIM, STOP HIM! KILL HIM!
NO MORE ORDERS, MINISTER! NOT TODAY...
...NOT EVER!

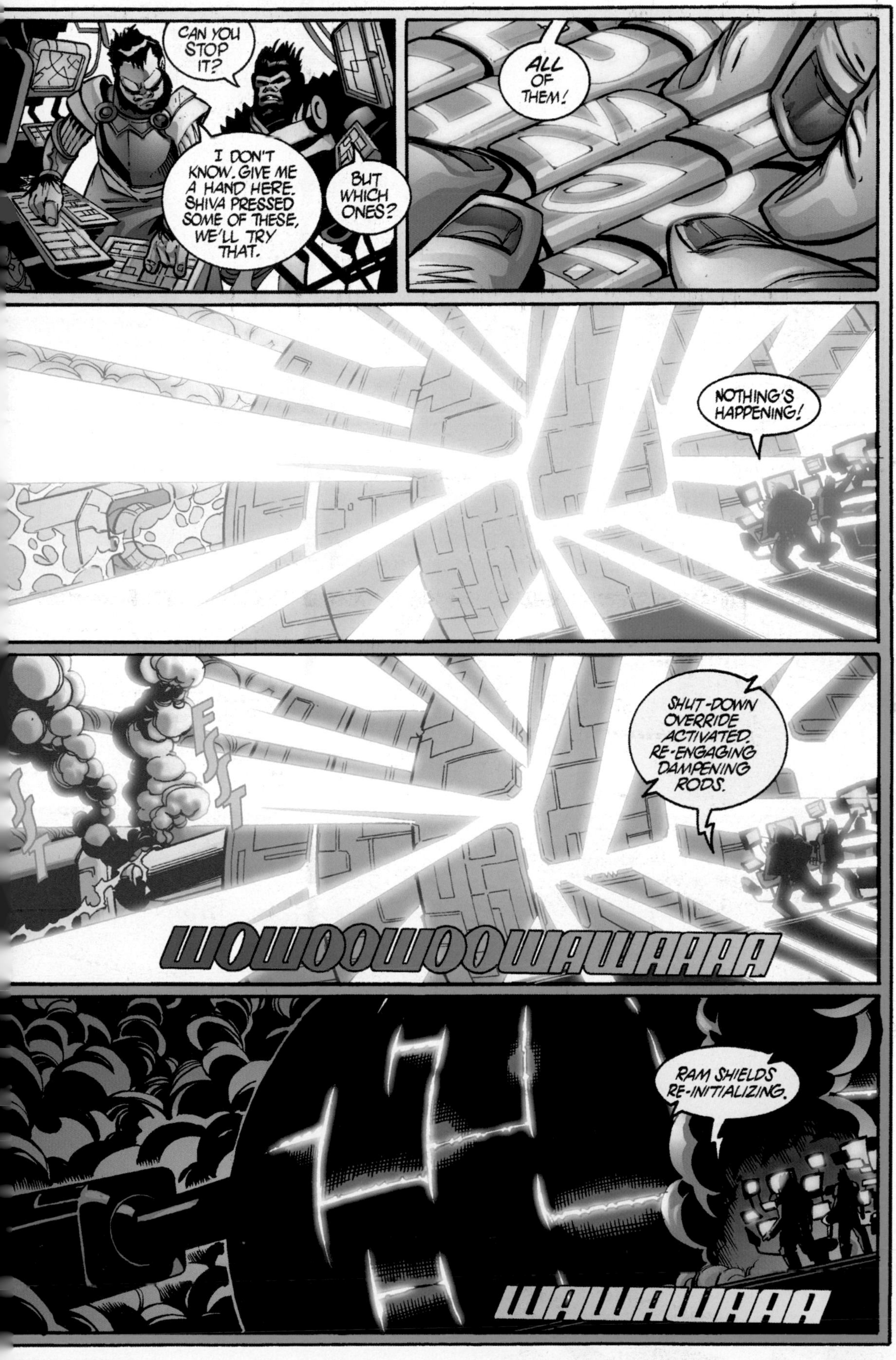
CAN YOU STOP IT?
I DON'T KNOW. GIVE ME A HAND HERE. SHIVA PRESSED SOME OF THESE, WE'LL TRY THAT.
BUT WHICH ONES?
ALL OF THEM!
NOTHING'S HAPPENING!
SHUT-DOWN OVERRIDE ACTIVATED. RE-ENGAGING DAMPENING RODS.
FSST
WOWOOWOOWAWAAAA
RAM SHIELDS RE-INITIALIZING.
WAWAWAAR

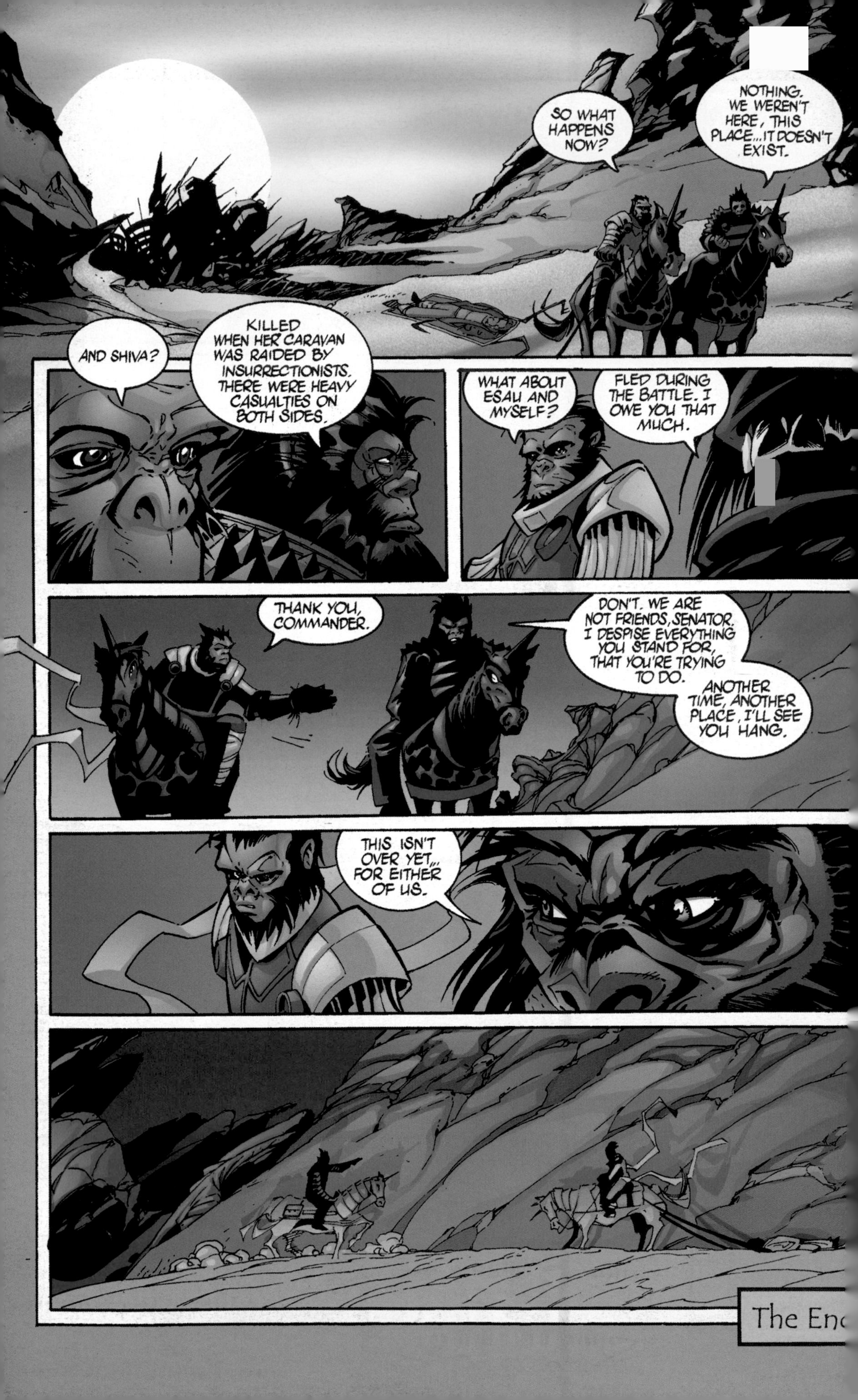
SO WHAT HAPPENS NOW?
NOTHING. WE WEREN'T HERE, THIS PLACE... IT DOESN'T EXIST.
AND SHIVA?
KILLED WHEN HER CARAVAN WAS RAIDED BY INSURRECTIONISTS. THERE WERE HEAVY CASUALTIES ON BOTH SIDES.
WHAT ABOUT ESAU AND MYSELF?
FLED DURING THE BATTLE. I OWE YOU THAT MUCH.
THANK YOU, COMMANDER.
DON'T. WE ARE NOT FRIENDS, SENATOR. I DESPISE EVERYTHING YOU STAND FOR, THAT YOU'RE TRYING TO DO.
ANOTHER TIME, ANOTHER PLACE, I'LL SEE YOU HANG.
THIS ISN'T OVER YET... FOR EITHER OF US.
The End

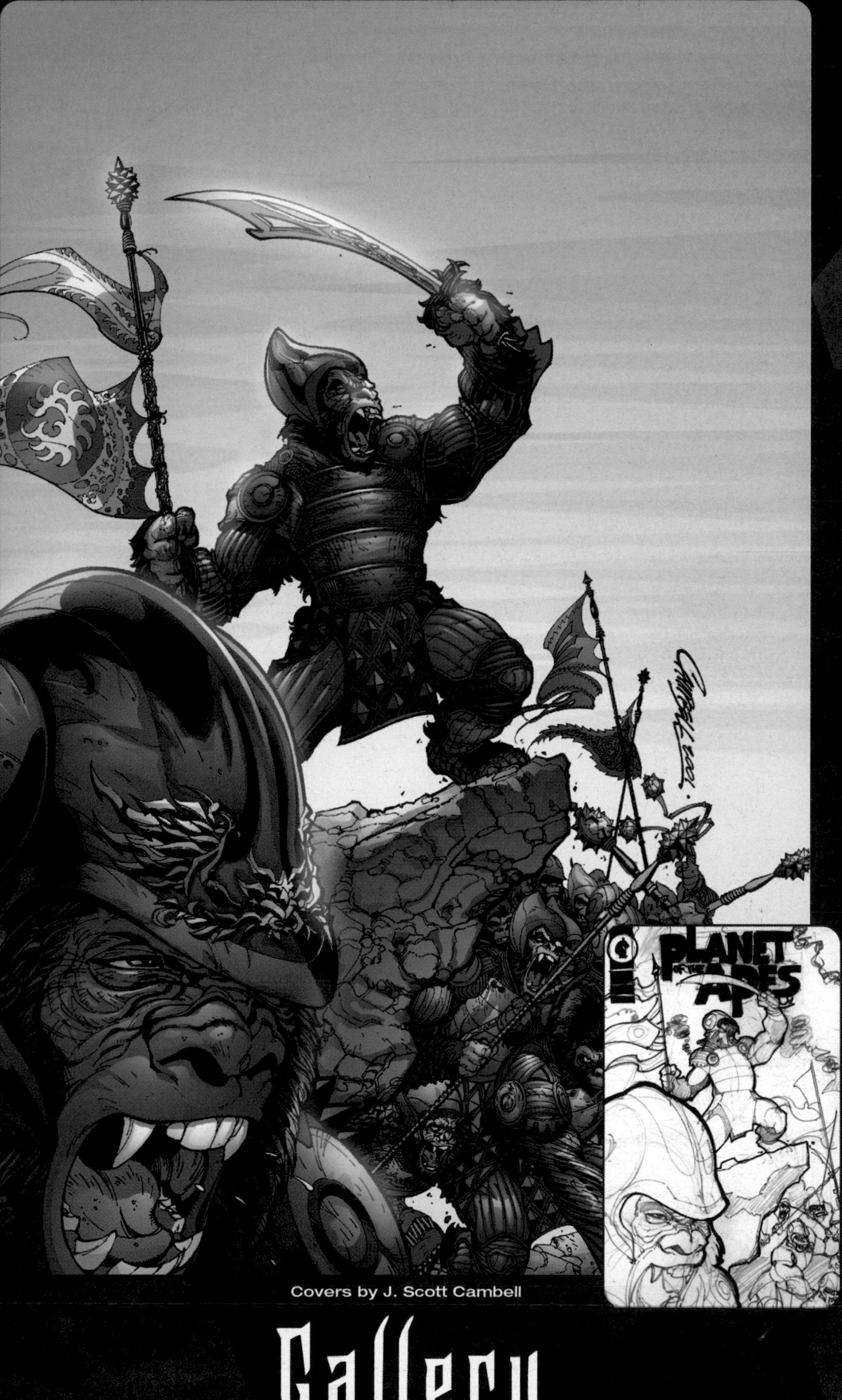
PLANET OF THE APES

Covers by J. Scott Cambell

Gallery

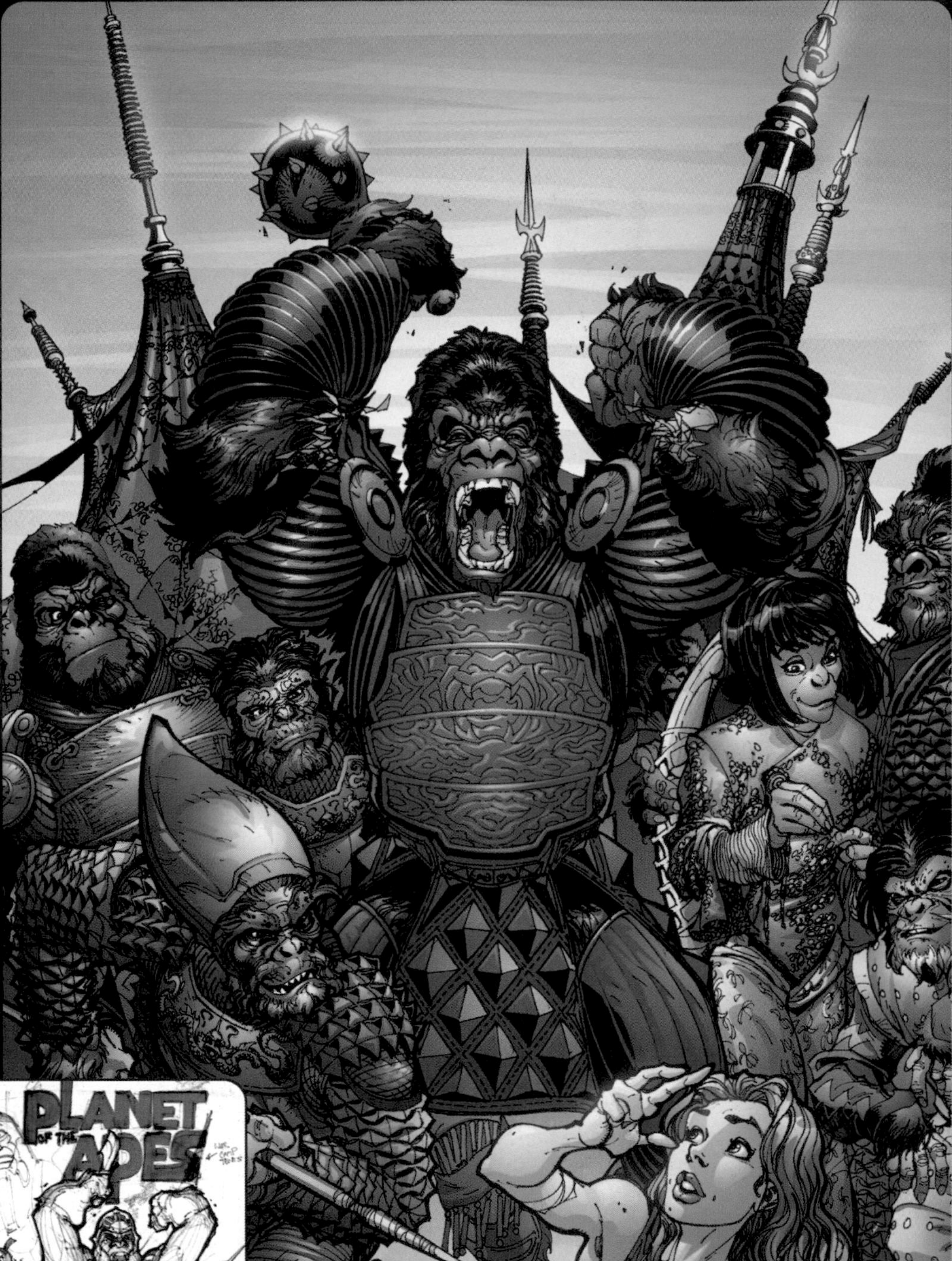
CAMPBELL 2001

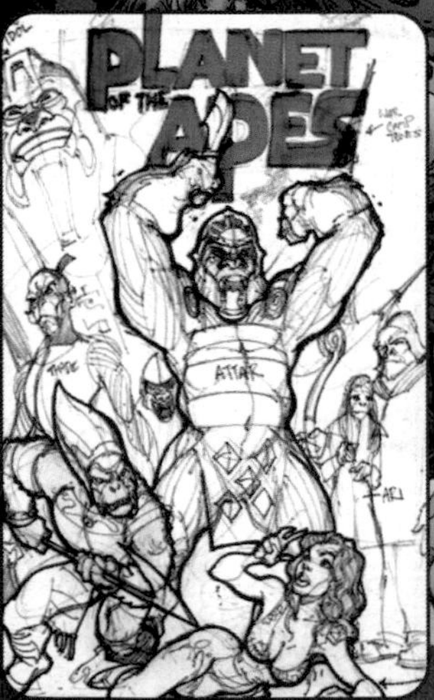
PLANET
OF THE
APES
ATTAR
ARI

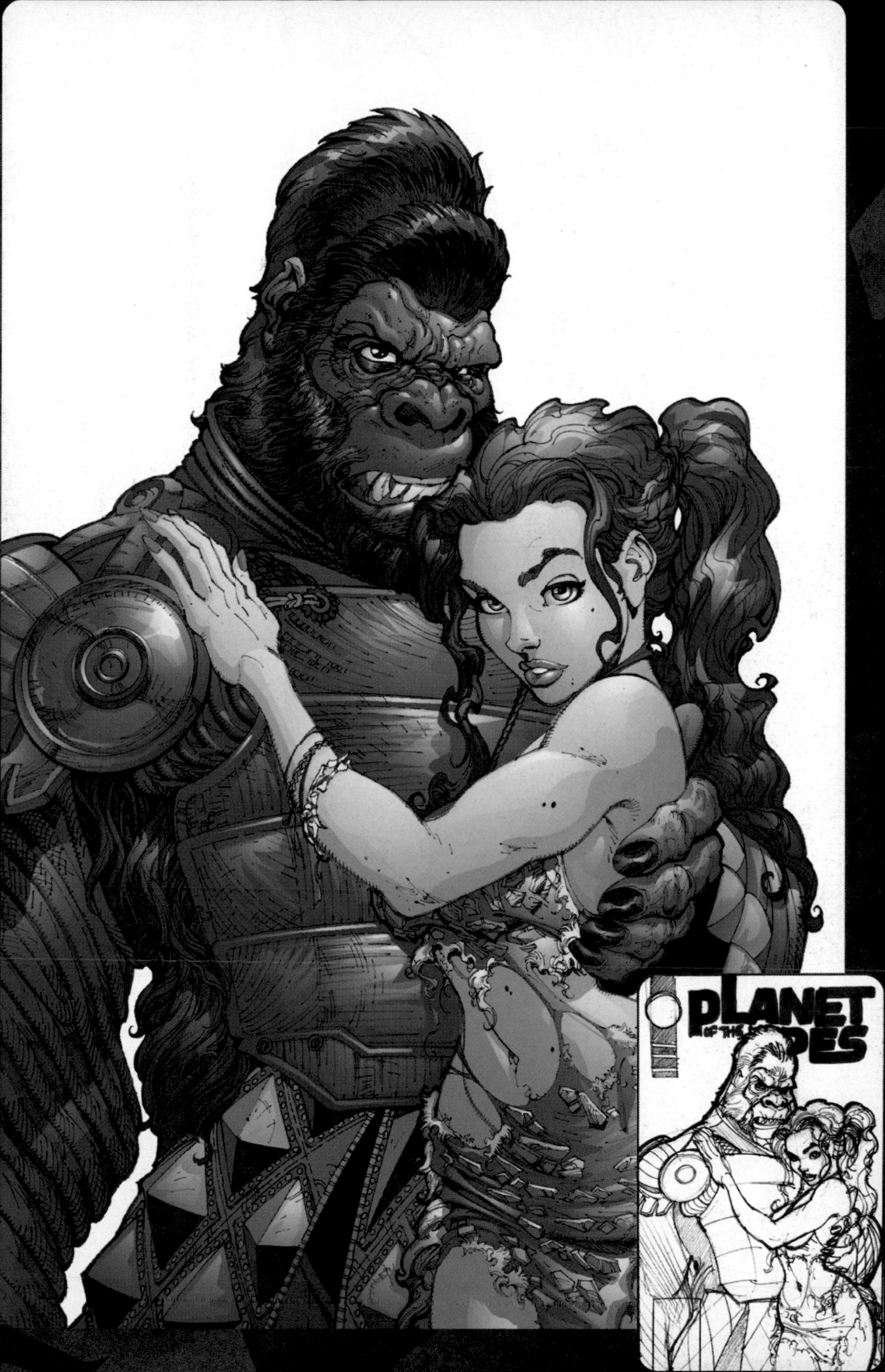
PLANET
OF THE
PES

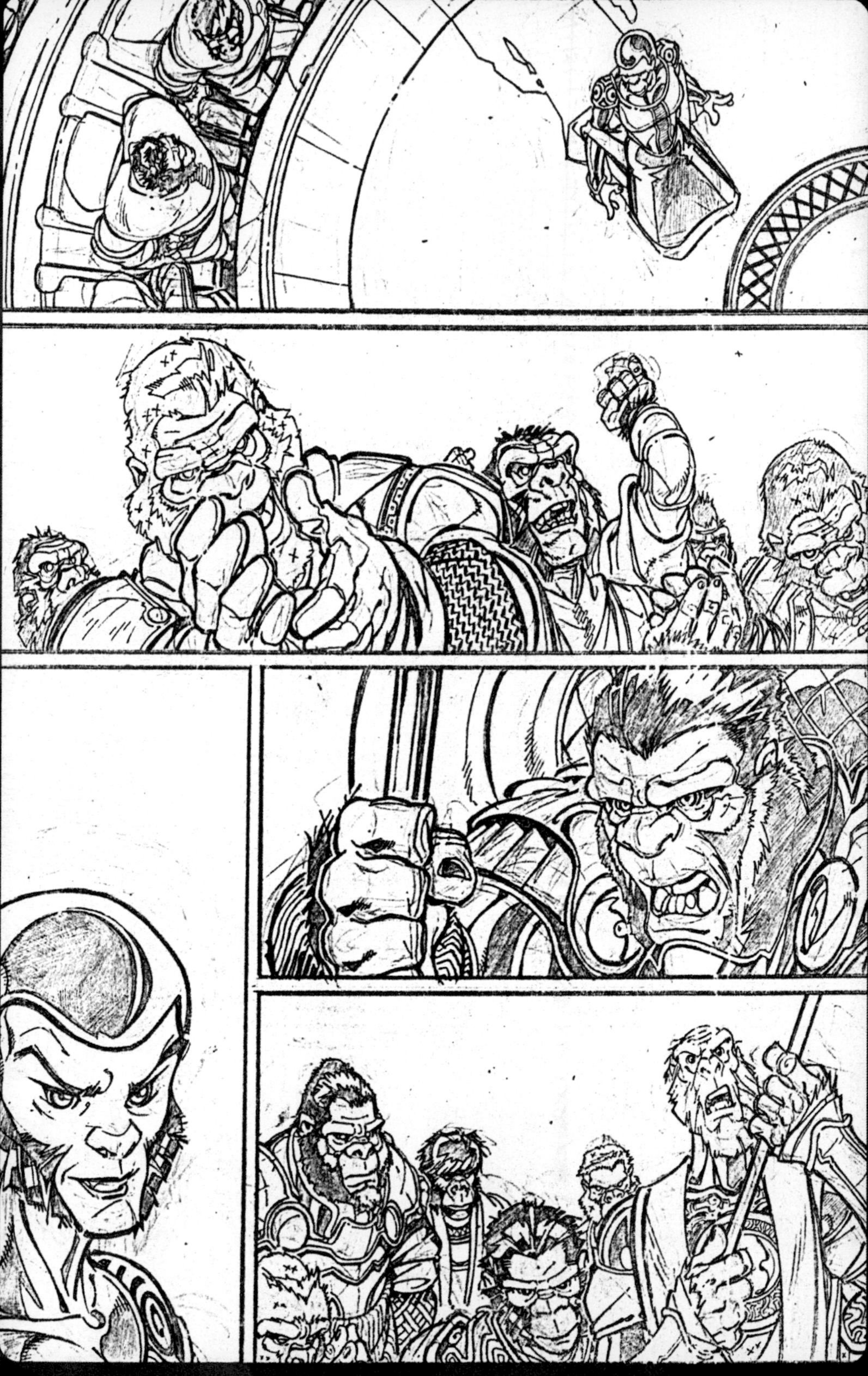

Paco Medina's pencil work for the series

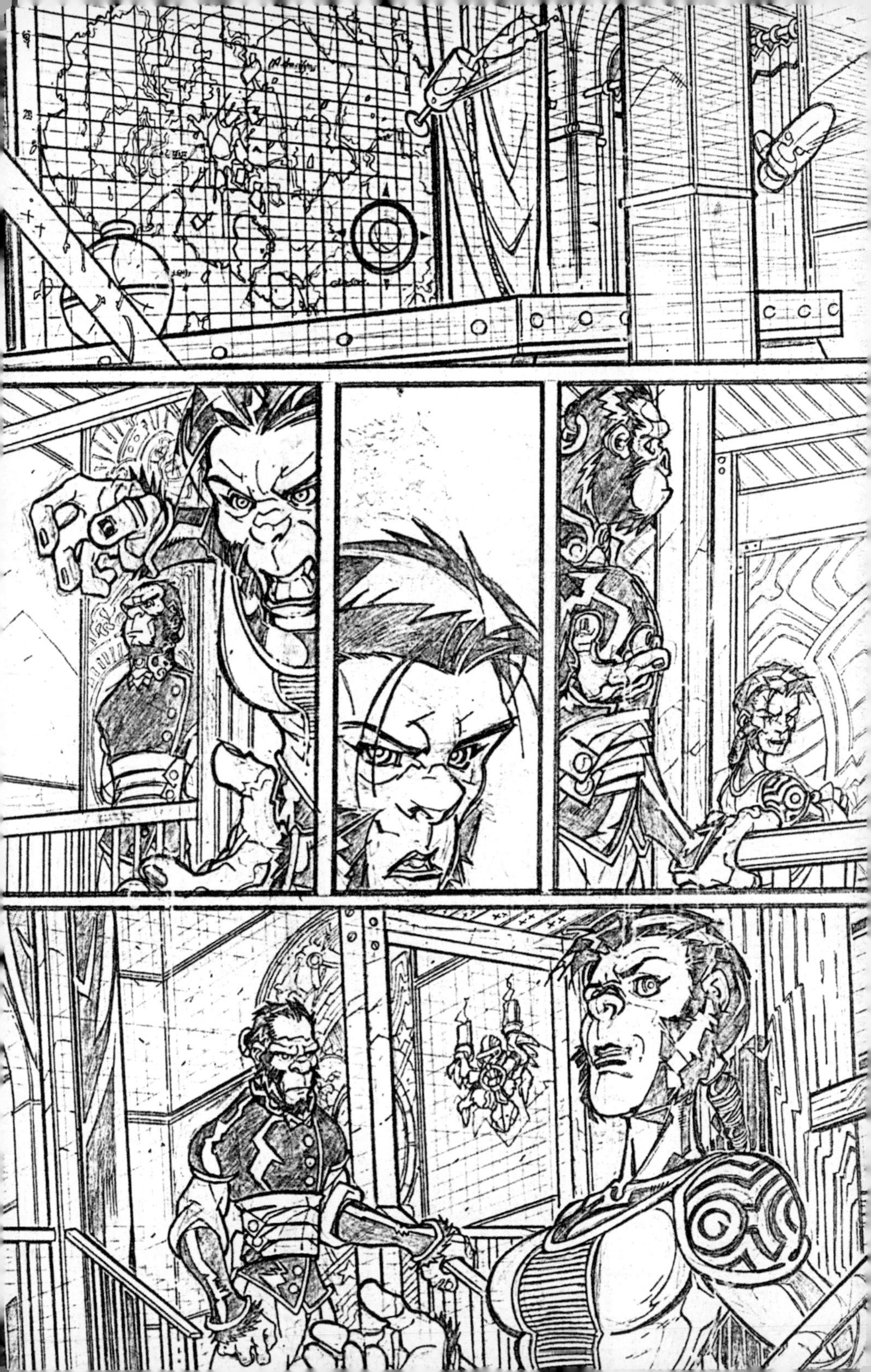

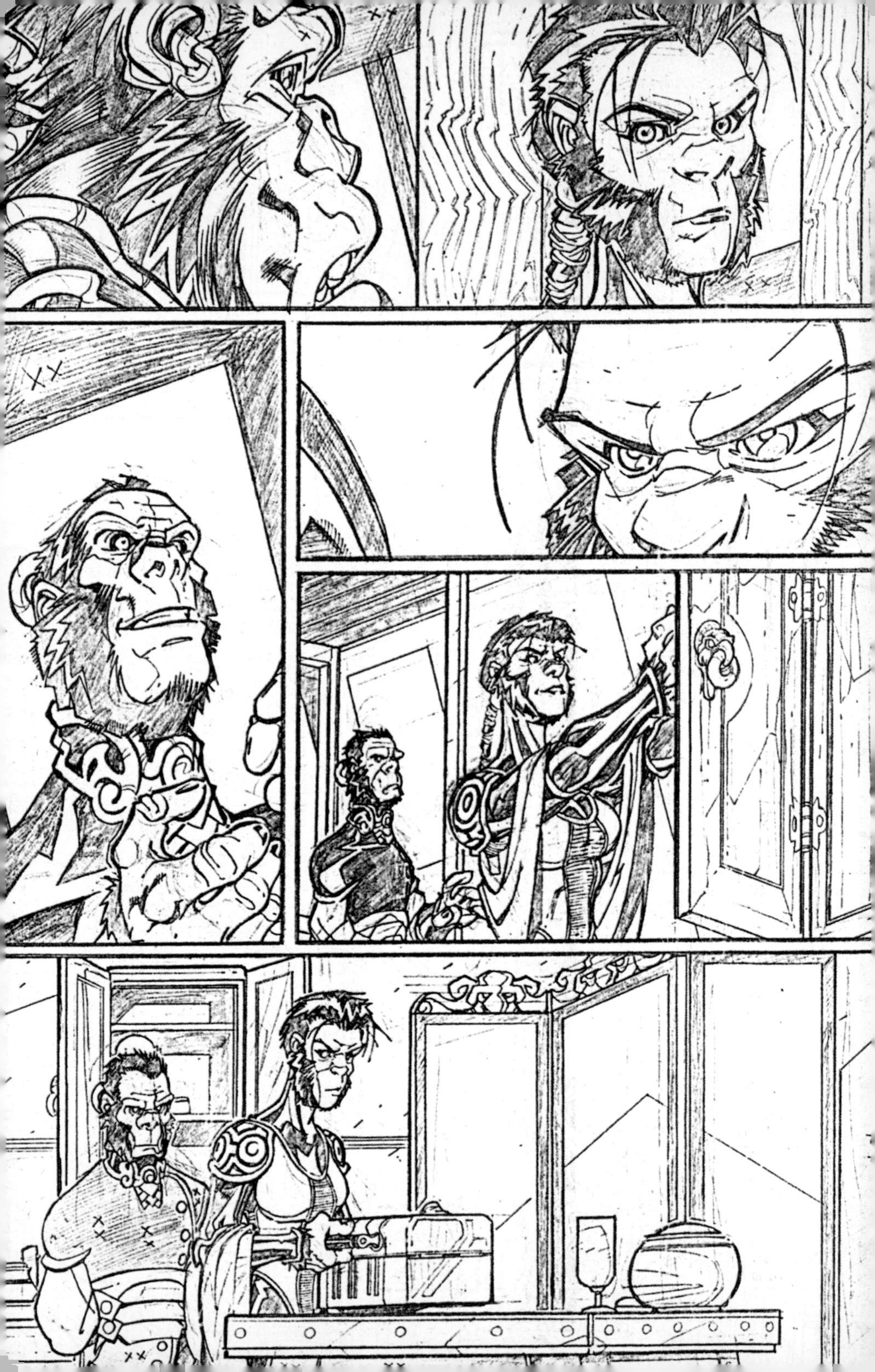

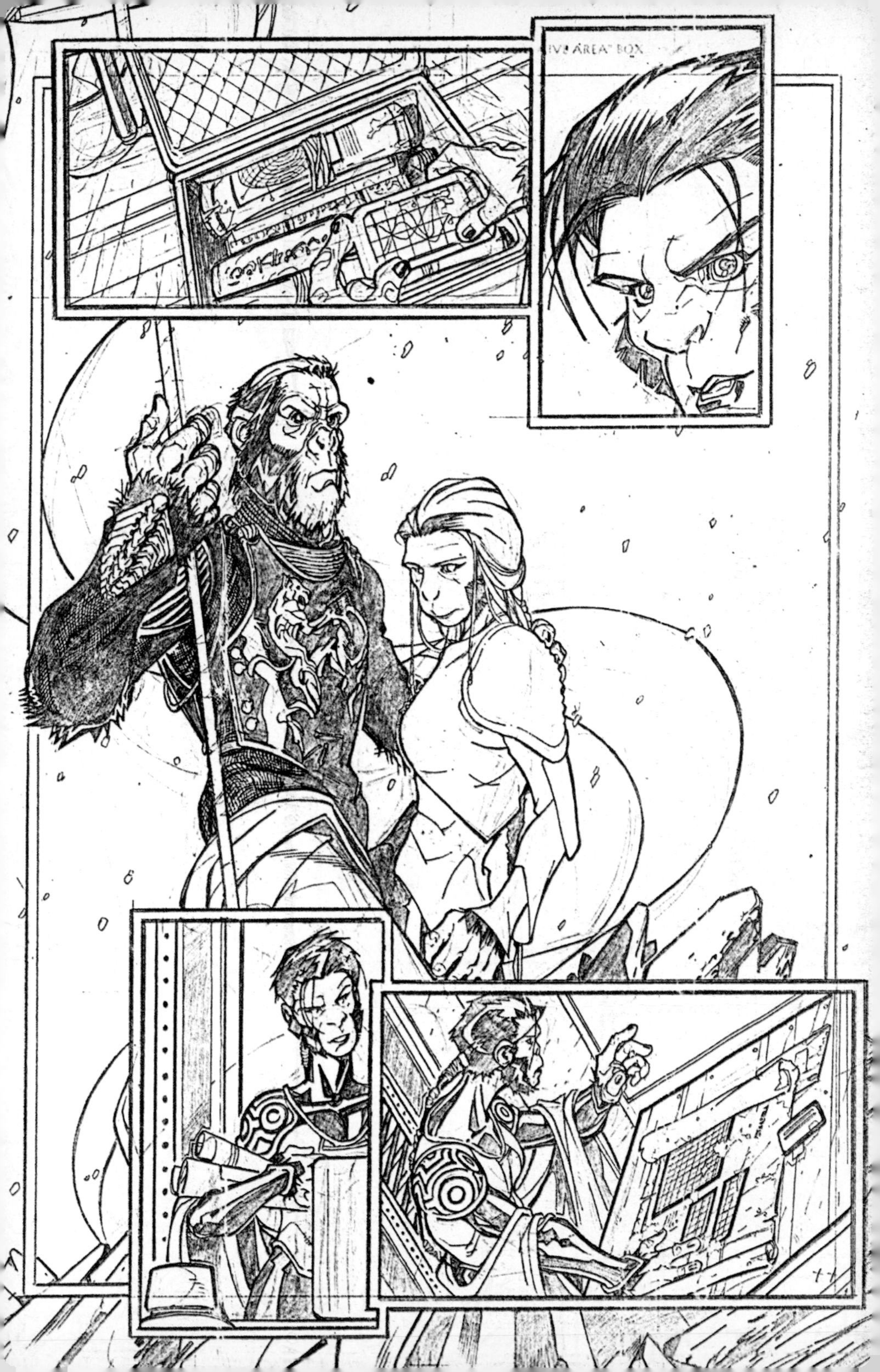

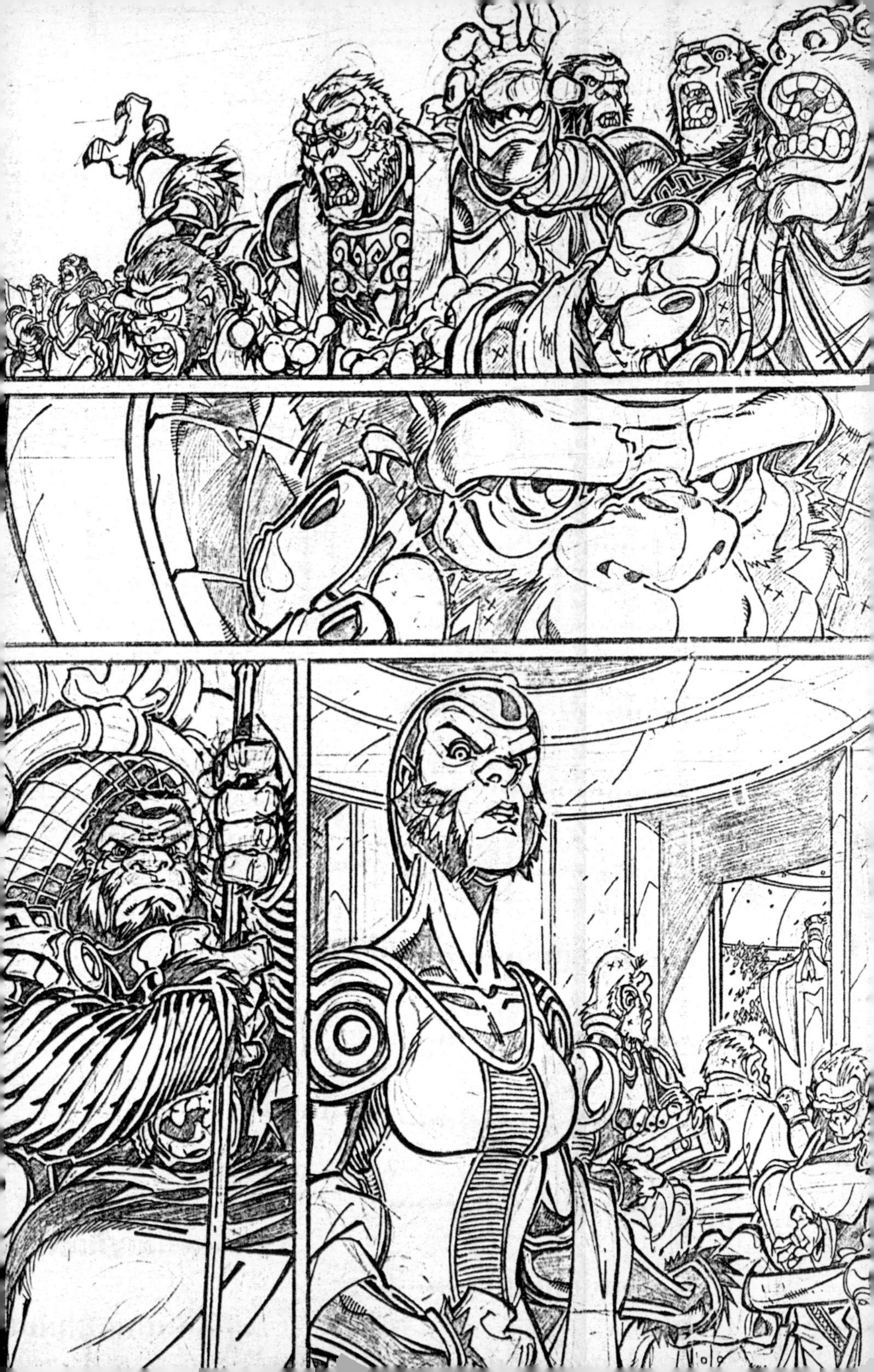

LOOK FOR THESE BUFFY THE VAMPIRE SLAYER TRADE PAPERBACKS FROM TITAN BOOKS.

The Dust Waltz
Brereton • Gomez • Florea
80-page color paperback
ISBN: 1-84023-057-6 **£7.99**

The Remaining Sunlight
Watson • Bennett • Ketcham
80-page color trde paperback
ISBN: 1-84023-078-9 **£7.99**

The Origin
Golden • Brereton • Bennett • Ketcham
80-page color paperback
ISBN: 1-84023-105-X **£7.99**

Uninvited Guests
Watson • Gomez • Florea
104-page color paperback
ISBN: 1-84023-140-8 **£8.99**

Supernatural Defense Kit
Watson • Richards • Pimentel
30-page color hard cover
comes with golden-colored cross,
"claddagh" ring, and vial of "Holy water"
ISBN: 1-84023-165-3 **£19.99**

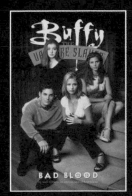

Bad Blood
Watson • Bennett • Ketcham
88-page color paperback
ISBN: 1-84023-179-3 **£8.99**

Crash Test Demons
Watson • Richards • Pimentel
88-page color paperback
ISBN: 1-84023-199-8 **£8.99**

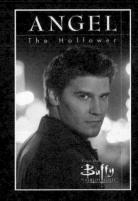

Angel: The Hollower
Golden • Gomez • Florea
88-page color paperback
ISBN: 1-84023-163-7 **£8.99**

Coming Soon!
Ring of Fire
Petrie • Sook
80-page color paperback
ISBN: 1-84023-200-5

Buffy the Vampire Slayer™ & Angel™ © Twentieth Century Fox Film Corporation. TM indicates a trademark of Twentieth Century Fox Film Corporation. All rights reserved.

All publications are available through most good bookshops or direct from our mail order service at Titan Books. For a free graphic-novels catalogue or to order, telephone 01858 433 169 with your credit-card details or contact Titan Books Mail Order, Bowden House, 36 Northampton Road, Market Harborough, Leics, LE16 9HE, quoting reference POTA/AW

www.buffy.com

ALIENS
LABYRINTH
Woodring • Plunkett
136-page color paperback
ISBN: 1-85286-844-9
NIGHTMARE ASYLUM
(formerly Aliens: Book Two)
Verheiden • Beauvais
112-page color paperback
ISBN: 1-85286-765-5
OUTBREAK
(formerly Aliens: Book One)
Verheiden • Nelson
168-page color paperback
ISBN: 1-85286-756-6
ALIENS VS PREDATOR
ALIENS VS PREDATOR
Stradley • Norwood • Warner
176-page color paperback
ISBN: 1-85286-413-3
**THE DEADLIEST
OF THE SPECIES**
Claremont • Guice • Barreto
320-page color paperback
ISBN: 1-85286-953-4
WAR
Various
200-page color paperback
ISBN: 1-85286-703-5
ETERNAL
Edginton • Maleev
88-page color paperback
ISBN: 1-84023-111-4
**ALIENS VS. PREDATOR
VS. TERMINTAOR**
Schultz • Ruby • Ivy
96-page color paperback
ISBN: 1-84023-313-3
ANGEL
THE HOLLOWER
Golden • Gomez • Florea
88-page color paperback
ISBN: 1-84023-163-7
SURROGATES
Golden •Zanier •
Owens • Gomez
80-page color paperback
ISBN: 1-84023-234-X
BUFFY THE VAMPIRE SLAYER
THE DUST WALTZ
Brereton • Gomez
80-page color paperback
ISBN: 1-84023-057-6
THE REMAINING SUNLIGHT
Watson • Van Meter •
Bennett • Ross
88-page color paperback
ISBN: 1-84023-078-9
THE ORIGIN
Golden • Brereton •
Bennett • Ketcham
80-page color paperback
ISBN: 1-84023-105-X
RING OF FIRE
Petrie • Sook
80-page color paperback
ISBN: 1-84023-200-5
UNINVITED GUESTS
Watson • Brereton •
Gomez • Florea
96-page color paperback
ISBN: 1-84023-140-8

BAD BLOOD
Watson • Bennett • Ketcham
88-page color paperback
ISBN: 1-84023-179-3
CRASH TEST DEMONS
Watson • Richards • Pimentel
88-page color paperback
ISBN: 1-84023-199-8
PALE REFLECTIONS
Watson • Richards • Pimentel
96-page color paperback
ISBN: 1-84023-236-6
THE BLOOD OF CARTHAGE
Golden • Richards • Pimentel
128-page color paperback
ISBN: 1-84023-281-1
STAR WARS
**BOBA FETT: ENEMY OF
THE EMPIRE**
Wagner • Gibson • Nadeau
112-page color paperback
ISBN: 1-84023-125-4
BOUNTY HUNTERS
Stradley • Truman • Schultz •
Mangels •Nadeau • Rubi • Saltares
112-page color paperback
ISBN: 1-84023-238-2
CHEWBACCA
Macan • Various
96-page color paperback
ISBN: 1-84023-274-9
CRIMSON EMPIRE
Richardson • Stradley •
Gulacy • Russell
160-page color paperback
ISBN: 1-84023-006-1
CRIMSON EMPIRE II
Richardson • Stradley •
Gulacy • Emberlin
160-page color paperback
ISBN: 1-84023-126-2
DARK EMPIRE
Veitch • Kennedy
184-page color paperback
ISBN: 1-84023-098-3
DARK EMPIRE II
Veitch • Kennedy
168-page color paperback
ISBN: 1-84023-099-1
**EPISODE I
THE PHANTOM MENACE**
Gilroy • Damaggio • Williamson
112-page color paperback
ISBN: 1-84023-025-8
EPISODE I ADVENTURES
152-page color paperback
ISBN: 1-84023-177-7
JEDI ACADEMY – LEVIATHAN
Anderson • Carrasco • Heike
96-page color paperback
ISBN: 1-84023-138-6
THE LAST COMMAND
Baron • Biukovic • Shanower
144-page color paperback
ISBN: 1-84023-007-X
**MARA JADE:
BY THE EMPEROR'S HAND**
Zahn • Stackpole • Ezquerra
144-page color paperback
ISBN: 1-84023-011-8

PRELUDE TO REBELLION
Strnad • Winn • Jones
144-page color paperback
ISBN: 1-84023-139-4
SHADOWS OF THE EMPIRE
Wagner • Plunkett • Russell
160-page color paperback
ISBN: 1-84023-009-6
**SHADOWS OF THE EMPIRE:
EVOLUTION**
Perry • Randall • Simmons
120-page color paperback
ISBN: 1-84023-135-1
**TALES OF THE JEDI:
DARK LORDS OF THE SITH**
Veitch • Anderson • Gossett
160-page color paperback
ISBN: 1-84023-129-7
**TALES OF THE JEDI:
FALL OF THE SITH**
Anderson • Heike • Carrasco, Jr.
136-page color paperback
ISBN: 1-84023-012-6
**TALES OF THE JEDI: THE
GOLDEN AGE OF THE SITH**
Anderson • Gossett •
Carrasco • Heike
144-page color paperback
ISBN: 1-84023-000-2
**TALES OF THE JEDI:
THE SITH WAR**
152-page color paperback
ISBN: 1-84023-130-0
UNION
Stackpole • Teranishi • Chuckry
96-page color paperback
ISBN: 1-84023-233-1
VADER'S QUEST
Macan • Gibbons • McKie
96-page color paperback
ISBN: 1-84023-149-1
**X-WING ROGUE SQUADRON:
THE WARRIOR PRINCESS**
Stackpole • Tolson •
Nadeau • Ensign
96-page color paperback
ISBN: 1-85286-997-6
**X-WING ROGUE SQUADRON:
REQUIEM FOR A ROGUE**
Stackpole • Strnad • Erskine
112-page color paperback
ISBN: 1-84023-026-6
**X-WING ROGUE SQUADRON:
IN THE EMPIRE'S SERVICE**
Stackpole • Nadeau • Ensign
96-page color paperback
ISBN: 1-84023-008-8
**X-WING ROGUE SQUADRON:
BLOOD AND HONOR**
Stackpole • Crespo •
Hall • Johnson
96-page color paperback
ISBN: 1-84023-010-X
**X-WING ROGUE SQUADRON:
MASQUERADE**
Stackpole •Johnson • Martin
96-page color paperback
ISBN: 1-84023-201-3
**X-WING ROGUE SQUADRON:
MANDATORY RETIREMENT**
Stackpole • Crespo • Nadeau
96-page color paperback
ISBN: 1-84023-239-0

All publications are available through most good bookshops or
direct from our mail-order service at Titan Books. For a free
graphic-novels catalogue or to order, telephone 01858 433 169
with your credit-card details or contact Titan Books Mail Order,
Bowden House, 36 Northampton Road, Market Harborough, Leics,
LE16 9HE, quoting reference POTA/AW.